Ingram
08/30
25—

NEW ENGLAND
NOTEBOOK

Mt. Mansfield, Stowe, Vermont

NEW ENGLAND
NOTEBOOK

One Reporter, Six States, Uncommon Stories

TED REINSTEIN

Guilford, Connecticut

All photographs by Ted Reinstein unless otherwise noted

Project Editor: Tracee Williams
Design and layout: Maggie Peterson
Map © Morris Book Publishing, LLC

Library of Congress Cataloging-in-Publication Data

Reinstein, Ted.
 New England notebook : one reporter, six states, uncommon stories / Ted Reinstein.
    pages cm
 Includes index.
 ISBN 978-0-7627-7841-6 (alkaline paper)
 1. New England—Description and travel—Anecdotes. 2. Reinstein, Ted—Travel—New England—
Anecdotes. 3. New England—History, Local—Anecdotes. 4. New England—Social life and cus-
toms—Anecdotes. 5. New England—Biography—Anecdotes. I. Title.
 F10.R45 2013
 974—dc23
                                                                                    2012050361

Printed in the United States of America

10 9 8 7 6 5 4 3 2 1

With love to Anne-Marie, Kyra, and Daisy

Cape Neddick ("Nubble") Lighthouse, York, Maine Photo courtesy of Vera Kaufman

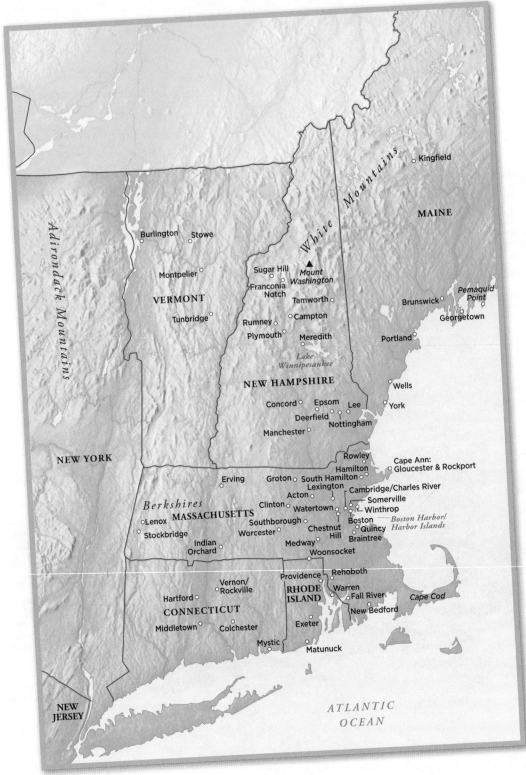

New England

CONTENTS

PREFACE: WORKING MY WAY AROUND NEW ENGLAND

I was born in Boston and raised in Winthrop, Massachusetts, a small (just over a square mile) but thickly settled seaside town that juts out into Boston Harbor. I moved away, have lived and traveled elsewhere, and in time, returned to Massachusetts (though, alas, farther away from the ocean). But nowhere have I loved where I live like New England.

At the bottom of his own love song to America, "This Land Is Your Land," Woody Guthrie wrote, "All you can write is what you see." Others have phrased the same sentiment differently. Then there's humorist P. J. O'Rourke's perspective: "The blind guy with the funny little harp who composed the *Iliad*—how much combat do you think he saw?"

What's certain for me is that I've seen more of New England than anywhere else. And through my work and my own odysseys around the region, I've been fortunate in getting to know it pretty well, too. No funny little harp for me, though, but rather a notebook (not to mention a microphone and camera), and the trusted company of talented videographers. In reporting for the Boston-based television newsmagazine, *Chronicle*, I've carried on a small part of what this unique and celebrated show has done faithfully, five nights a week, for thirty years: tell the stories of New England. From Rhode Island to Rangeley Lake, Stonington to Stowe, Kenmore Square to Kinsman Notch, I've traveled all over New England's six states, from its cities, to smaller towns, to mere dots on a map. From the seacoast to the mountains, and all the filled-up flatland in between, we've passed mile after mile, meeting folks and finding things out in every corner of New England. Along bustling urban streets and hushed wooded trails, in farm fields and working waterfronts, in places of play and politics, of work and worship . . . and in places of wonderment, simply, sometimes, at what the earth has wrought in rugged beauty here.

Like coming around the famed, "Oh, my God" curve on Route 27 in Kingfield, Maine, for the first time. Suddenly the massive bulk and breadth that is Sugarloaf Mountain filled my view, like a stand-alone, snow-capped kingdom thrust up from the earth. I hit the brakes, dropped my jaw, and sure enough, found myself exhaling quietly, as if on cue, "Oh, my God. . . ."

But we've also followed New England's stories far from the photo ops and the Currier & Ives postcard scenes. In the shadow of those mountains, or hugging the seacoast and river valleys, are hardworking ports and cities and tired old mill towns that have struggled to sustain and reinvent themselves. Then there's the penchant New Englanders have for playing outside, cracking jokes, collecting things, and cooking up some pretty delicious foods. Those stories stand out, too.

From all of my travels, I'm left with one overall impression: As strikingly diverse as the physical New England landscape is, so are its people. In a way, New Englanders mirror their region's fabled weather: complex, varied, tough to predict, frequently changing, full of extremes. (Mark Twain, who spent over thirty years in New England, said of its weather, "If you don't like it, wait a minute.")

That same endless change and variety about life in New England is what's impressed me most in my travels. What follows are some of those stories. And while they're literally all over the map, they do have one thing in common: They're my favorites.

Pemaquid Point Lighthouse, Bristol, Maine Photo courtesy of Vera Kaufman

CHAPTER 1

THE OLDEST
What's So New about New England?

If states were people, the six New England states would be the nation's wizened, white-haired seniors, shuffling around up there in the nation's northeast corner, cupping their ears while trading tall tales about the War of Independence or the Blizzard of '88. 1888. New England was already the "nation's attic" well before the Smithsonian called itself that. Relics of history and tradition are scattered about New England like old-fashioned furnishings and outdated appliances: low, stone walls in the woods where cows once grazed; crooked, creaking, wooden piers that once tied up square-rigged sailing ships; rows of faded, brick mill buildings that once hummed, harnessed rivers, and produced textiles for a young and growing nation. Consider the birth order among the family of American states. When Alaska and Hawaii became the forty-ninth and fiftieth states in 1959, almost two *centuries* had passed since Massachusetts had become the nation's sixth state. That's like a two-hundred-year age difference between siblings. No, there's nothing "new" about New England, except of course, to settlers from "olde" England, which had become a unified country more than *eight* centuries before they crossed the Atlantic. Age really is relative, isn't it?

Of course, if we go further back in history, the physical *place* that is New England was inhabited long, long before the English and the Pilgrims set foot there. Today, so many of the region's most colorful names—Nantucket, Narragansett, Pequot, Passamaquoddy, and Massachusetts itself—are traced to the region's natives and to large, tribal nations like the Penobscot and the Wampanoag. And while I've visited sites of native history and present-day tribal meeting places, met tribal leaders and done stories on descendants, New England's natives, unlike its newcomers, left little lasting, physical legacy. Therefore, most things we refer to as "oldest" in New England are, by this default, connected only with *European* settlement.

Boston: Oldest of the Old

Standard guidebooks gush about Boston's rich and colorful history. ("Walk the Freedom Trail in America's Cradle of Liberty!") As guidebook gushing goes, it's more or less accurate. Founded in 1630, just ten years after the Pilgrims established their colony in Plymouth, "The Hub" is New England's largest city, and has preserved much of its history remarkably well, while integrating the contemporary and the modern. For those who live or work around the city, the wood and brick of colonial-era buildings like Faneuil Hall and the Old South Meeting House blend seamlessly with the steel and glass of modern office towers. It's routine to dart across busy State Street, past the colonial-era Old State House, and over the raised cobblestones of the Boston Massacre site. Or hunt (usually in vain) for parking along Fort Point Channel and the location of the former Griffin's Wharf and the Boston Tea Party. Boston Common (America's oldest public park) still bustles with activity and festivals. And while perhaps it's progress that grazing a cow on the Common is no longer legal, it's definitely progress that a public hanging has not occurred there since 1817.

Old State House, State Street, Boston

"Listen My Children and You Shall Hear . . ." (About Paul Revere's Expense Report)

In some ways, the legacy of Paul Revere is ubiquitous in the Boston area. There's his house, his statue (on a horse, of course), and the city outside Boston that bears his name. But one of my favorite Revere legacies is tucked away in a vault. Casual visitors to Boston or those walking the city's Freedom Trail will never see it. We stumbled on it years ago doing a story on just that subject—interesting things scattered around the city that are largely hidden from the public view.

Few figures in American history are as legendary as Paul Revere. His "Midnight Ride," immortalized by Henry Wadsworth Longfellow, is a part of how generations of American schoolchildren know about Lexington, Concord, and the beginnings of American independence. (History doesn't record how many of those rudely awakened villagers no doubt first responded with, "Who the hell is making that racket in the middle of night?!")

Not only was Paul Revere a heroic patriot, he was also a talented artisan and silversmith whose creations were prized even in his own day. Nonetheless, he didn't have the Harvard cachet or upperclass Boston background (not to mention the wealth) of

Paul Revere Statue,
North End, Boston
Photo by Michael Keiloch

contemporaries like John Hancock, Joseph Warren, or James Otis. In addition, he had five kids and an elderly mother living at home with him and his wife in cramped quarters. When it came to work and income, he needed to be enterprising, practical, creative, and determined. And he was. In the wake of the Boston Massacre, for example, Revere turned out an engraving, which was then reproduced in handbills and broadsides of the period.

"It was sort of a tabloid photo of its time, meant to inflame anger against the British," says Massachusetts state archivist Michael Comeau. "The man had bills to pay."

Exhibit A? Paul Revere's—and perhaps America's earliest—expense report.

"Paul Revere's Bill" is part of the extensive collection in the Massachusetts State Archives at Columbia Point (a sprawling spit of land just south of downtown that includes UMass/Boston and the John F. Kennedy Presidential Library). Revere's bill to "The Colony of Massachusetts Bay," in part, reads:

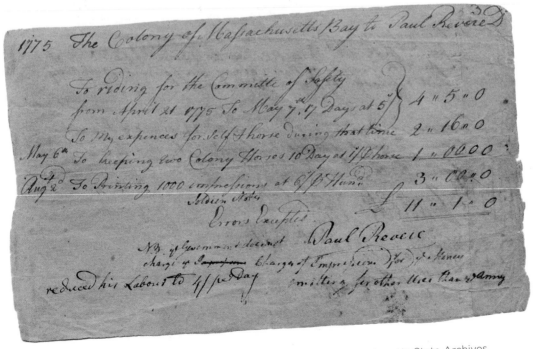

America's first expense report? Photo courtesy of Massachusetts State Archives

To Riding for the Committee of Safety, from April 21, 1775 to May 7th, 17 days at 5 sh. (sic, "shillings") . . . to my expenses for self and horse during that time . . . May 6th to keeping two colony horses 10 days at 1/sh horse . . .

In the same bill, Revere also sought to be reimbursed for the cost of printing "1000 impressions" (for soldiers' pay notes), but that was disallowed by Massachusetts's House of Representatives. (What present-day employee who's ever filed an expense report can't relate to Revere's early but irritating experience with those ever-balky bean counters?) On the other hand, on August 22, 1775, the House did approve the bulk of Paul Revere's expenses and, in the spirit of Revere's own frugality, they used the reverse side of the very same piece of paper on which he submitted the bill itself:

Resolved that Mr. Paul Revere be allowed and paid out of the public treasury of this colony ten pounds, four shillings in full discharge of the written account . . . Sent up for concurrence, Jas. Warren, Speaker . . . read and concurred, Saml. Adams, Secretary . . .

"Paul Revere was trying to make a buck, and his time was money," reminds Comeau.

"Did he pad the bill a little bit?" I wonder.

"Sure, he might have tried to pad it a bit," smiles Comeau.

Ultimately, though, Comeau sees the expense report as adding to, not diminishing the way we view Paul Revere.

"We wouldn't otherwise have seen this side of this historical figure. I like the fact it lets us see a real person behind the icon, who had real day-to-day financial concerns, just like most of us."

At least Revere did get mostly reimbursed. He might have had a tougher time of it today. In present-day dollars, Paul Revere's bill would have come out to roughly $1,081.87. Still, it seems like a reasonable price for a down payment on liberty. Besides, you try finding a free messenger at midnight.

Clinton Wins (No, Not That Clinton)

Fenway Park, which opened in 1912, is the oldest active Major League ballpark. But forty miles west of Boston, there's another ball field that is older still—by more than three full decades. In fact, the town of Clinton, Massachusetts, prides itself on being home to something virtually every other American city and town would envy like little else: the oldest baseball field. Anywhere.

Not that they go overboard about it in Clinton. Quite the opposite. A visitor to Fuller Field has to walk behind the chain-link backstop to even see the single, small sign: THE WORLD'S OLDEST BASEBALL DIAMOND. In 2007, the *Guinness Book of World Records* made it official. Yes, there are baseball fields and parks elsewhere that were built earlier, but according to *Guinness,* nowhere else has baseball been played continuously, year after year, in the same location, for a longer period of time.

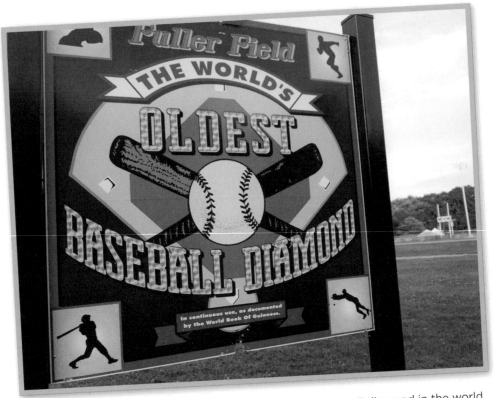

Clinton, Massachusetts: The oldest continuously used baseball diamond in the world

"Thank goodness someone saved that," Clinton native Terry Ingano tells me as we look at an old, yellowed map spread out on a table at the Clinton Historical Society. The 1878 map, long-forgotten in a town hall closet, clearly shows a baseball diamond, "Clinton Baseball Grounds," in the same location where the field exists today. The map proved decisive for *Guinness* in confirming the "oldest" title. More than six generations of baseball players (including Ingano), from Little League to high school to semi-pros, helped attest to it, too. I help Ingano carefully put the map away.

"My wife laughs," I tell him, "but this is why I never throw anything out!"

We make our way outside in the sun and head to the field. We'd heard about the Clinton claim. It seemed unlikely. But here we are.

Clinton, like many other former New England mill towns, has seen better days. Where once there was a thriving industrial base and widespread prosperity, there's now some scattered high-tech companies and several smaller businesses. Coffee shops, a few antiques stores, a couple of gas stations. People commute elsewhere. You get by. Set alongside the Nashua River, the town is tidy, compact, with a big wide main street and its own little hilltop Central Park, with some beautifully sculpted fountains. Like most American communities in the late nineteenth century, Clinton had many small baseball lots scattered around town. But by 1878, a former circus grounds on an area in the north end of town, owned by Rufus Boynton and known as "the Plains," had become the premier playing field. The first "official" game on "Boynton's lot" was played on June 15, 1878. And baseball has been played there every summer since.

"No question, there are older parks around the country, no question," concedes Ingano as we walk across the outfield on a still and humid mid-August afternoon.

"But here, it's never stopped, never moved location, never changed."

A lone cicada buzzes as we make our way across the outfield grass. Ingano surveys Fuller Field with a mix of town pride and personal nostalgia. As a school kid, he played his share of innings here on an infield made cement-like in chilly New England early springs, then turned parched and dusty on hot August days like this one.

"Shortstop, second, third, mostly outfield in high school—I could play nearly every position," Ingano says matter-of-factly. "And I was mediocre at every one of them!"

His position today is superintendent of schools in Clinton. We sit in the small grandstand along the first baseline, looking out at the freshly cut green grass, the foul lines already chalked bright white for a game. Truth is, Fuller Field is nothing special to look at. There's nothing about it that stands out to passersby, or even invites a second look. There's nothing architecturally significant; there aren't even any dugouts. It's not included in any glossy tour guides. It's not home to a minor league team with a funny logo and a schedule full of wacky promotional events. It just sits there on High Street, a simple chain-link fence separating a blue-collar ball field from a largely blue-collar neighborhood.

"Where are the tour buses, Terry?" I wonder out loud, ribbing Ingano. "There should be hats, T-shirts, bumper stickers, souvenir baseballs!"

"I know, right?"

He smiles, picks at some grass, and squints as he looks out toward left field. "I should retire and do that."

The baseball has never stopped.

The late afternoon hazy quiet is broken by the sound of cars pulling up, doors opening and closing. Guys in baseball uniforms and sneakers are arriving for a 6:00 p.m., thirty-plus league game. As they pull equipment bags from car trunks, lace up cleats and start to stretch, I ask some of them if they're aware they're at the oldest continuously played-on baseball field in the world. A few know, mostly from the sign. Others, mostly from out of town and here for the first time, are amazed.

"Wow," a hefty guy marvels while strapping on catcher's gear. "That's pretty cool."

It is pretty cool.

Terry Ingano heads for his car.

"Hey, maybe we'll have T-shirts next time you're here!"

Maybe. For now, at this field where yet another first pitch is about to be thrown, there's just a simple sign behind home plate that makes clear what no other frills around the field could embellish: THE WORLD'S OLDEST BASEBALL DIAMOND. And to sit in the small bleachers along the first base line on a warm summer night, and watch a local town league game drift toward dusk on a field where baseball has simply played on and on for over 130 years . . . well, put *that* on your T-shirt.

When the Antique Is the Antiques Store

America loves its "alleys." Not so much the city kind, but rather the big regional swaths that are famous for something, like tornadoes or alligators. In New Hampshire, it's antiques. The twenty-mile stretch of Route 4 between the traffic circles of Epsom and Lee is known as "Antique Alley." For good reason. On this stretch of rolling road, every bend seems to reveal another antiques sign, another clutch of wooden chairs, tin wash basins, and vintage mirrors arranged on the front porch or on the grass by the side of the road. Mile for mile, it's the highest concentration of antiques stores in America.

"You can't do the whole route in a day, I'll tell you that," assures Rich Bojko, who now owns Parker-French Antiques, site of the store that started it all back in 1976. Colleen Pingree, owner of the pink-and-impossible-to-miss R.S. Butler's Antiques, agrees. In fact, she won't even hazard a guess as to the literally uncountable volume of antiques overflowing her own place.

"Every once in a while we think about adding it up. But we don't."

Both Bojko and Pingree agree on the best way for us to capture the true flavor and essence of Antique Alley. They advise us to stop in at the Betty House, oldest of the area's actual buildings, and to visit with its owner, Charlie Yeaton, who they describe as Antique Alley's "Dealer Emeritus." Excellent advice, as it turns out.

The Betty House, we soon discover, does not actually sit on Antique Alley. We turn off of Route 4, continue on another smaller road, and then make our way up a hill and through the woods a bit. At a bend in the road, a huge, sagging old wooden barn faces us; on the other side of the road are the other three buildings that comprise the little antiques compound that is Charlie Yeaton's. Off to the side is Betty House itself, a three-hundred-year-old handsome white colonial in which Yeaton grew up. And then out pops Charlie himself. Yeaton, we also discover, is more active than emeritus. Way more. He's slight, wears a striped shirt with old blue jeans, and has short white hair, glasses, an impish grin, and an even more impish sense of things in general.

Betty House Antiques, circa early 1800s Photo courtesy of *Chronicle*/WCVB-TV

"You found us," he smiles. "Not everyone does, you know."

And not every eighty-something has Charlie Yeaton's energy or has worn as many hats. It's true he's retired from his nearly forty-year career as a public school teacher and principal. And he did decide not to seek reelection after his tenth term as a state representative. But there'll be no retiring from antiques.

"I've always been interested in antiques, brought up in a house built in the late 1700s, and the attic was full of stuff from previous generations." Yeaton speaks softly in a high-pitched voice; I lean in to hear better.

"I have many things in the shop that we used when we were kids," he laughs wryly. "Now most people don't know what they are."

As we walk over to a large shed-like building tucked in amongst the trees, I ask him what makes his own antiques place unique.

"It's not all neat and clean, the way some shops are," he says, swinging open an old door. "Some people object to that—matter of fact, they come in and look in the door, and leave in horror."

Charlie Yeaton Photo courtesy of *Chronicle*/WCVB-TV

I see what he means. Things are all over the place. There may be some system to it, but if so, it's not information Charlie Yeaton shares.

"These flashlights by the door don't look that old, Charlie."

"They're not," he says. "No lights in here, though, so they come in pretty handy for most folks."

But not to everyone.

"Some years back there was a woman here, and she was fumbling around by the door, and she said, 'Where's the light switch?' So I said to her that when they built this building, they didn't put in electricity, mostly because it hadn't been invented yet. She got a little irritated with me. Left shortly thereafter, actually."

We stay. We look through some great stuff, like the huge collection of earthenware jugs that Charlie surmises have held a whole lot of (very) hard cider over the years. In the big barn itself, I walk slowly through row after row of old wooden carpenter's tools. I stop in front of some faded, "Charlie Yeaton for State Rep." posters. He tells us he never had a campaign manager.

"Didn't need one," he chuckles.

He does, however, have a small forest of wooden chairs in the barn; they hang over us, in back of us, everywhere.

"So, Charlie, when people stop by and ask if you have any chairs, what do you say?"

"Oh, a few."

More browsing, and when we finally leave it's only because our schedule requires us to. I feel like my blood pressure has come down ten points over the past hour here. Maybe it's the quiet of the barns, the woods, the antiques. Maybe it's Charlie Yeaton. He's set himself in an old, creaking rocking chair by the barn door in the late afternoon sun as we say goodbye.

"It's not a big money-making thing, that's for sure," he says, smiling and smoothing out a spot on the chair's arm with his handkerchief. "But I meet a lot of nice people, have a lot of fun, and I guess I'm just sort of addicted to antiques."

I look in the rear view mirror as we slowly drive back down the hill. Charlie's already heading back into the barn to re-hang the rocking chair with the others.

Who's got time to sit?

OYSTERS AND HISTORY

Less than one hundred yards from Boston's newest public parkland (more on that ahead) lies a small triangle of street and storefront that has remained remarkably changeless for three centuries. On Marshall Street, if one's gaze stays fixed low on the cobblestones and building facades and avoids looking higher to see the surrounding modern city, it's possible to be entirely transported to Paul Revere's Boston. (His house is also a mere stone's throw away.) At the corner of Marshall and Union Streets is Boston's oldest standing brick building and the oldest restaurant (1826) in America, The Union Oyster House. Indeed, #41 Union is an address that's been extraordinarily well-brushed by the sweep of history: A full century before the first oyster was served here, it had already been a dry goods store, home of a future French king, rebel printing press (the British called the building the "Sedition Foundry"), and paymaster headquarters for George Washington's Continental Army. To sit at its legendary, semi-circular, soapstone raw bar is to be transported in time. It's easy to imagine the presence of earlier patrons like Daniel Webster who, as a legislator, would walk down daily from Beacon Hill and order dozens of oysters to

Marshall Street, view to Union Street, Boston

be washed down by several tumblers of brandy. (Try that on *your* lunch hour.) Owner Joe Milano, whose family has owned the Union Oyster House since 1970, is happy to point out the booths of other famous regulars, like former president John F. Kennedy.

"If only these walls could talk," smiles Milano.

Milano also loves to share a lesser-known historical footnote: In addition to being the haunt of future kings and presidents, The Union Oyster House is also home to the humble toothpick. In the late 1800s, the toothpick's inventor (and guerilla marketing pioneer) Charles Forster of Maine set up a sneaky little deal with local Harvard students: He'd buy them dinner if, afterward, they'd ask for toothpicks they knew in advance the restaurant did not yet stock—then complain loudly. In time, The Union Oyster House did indeed stock the newfangled toothpick. And the rest is, well, yet more history.

Raw Bar, Union Oyster House

CHAPTER 2

THE SMALLEST

Big Is for Lone Star, Not Ocean State

Look at the US map. Look out west at the size of behemoth states like California or Montana. Now gaze east at itty-bitty Massachusetts or Rhode Island. Sort of pitiful, isn't it? Course, Massachusetts does have nine US representatives to Montana's one. And to be fair, you can also get "oysters" in the Rockies. (Also known as "tendergroins" or "calf fries," they're definitely *not* related to the variety served at Union Oyster House.)

The truth is, if you follow out from New England with an eye on how the states become physically larger, you're really following the evolution of a growing nation. It's as if in the beginning, in New England, it was all the settlers could do to eke out a secure toehold from the rugged wilderness. Six toeholds. Hacked-out, roughly farmed patches of people and towns that became colonies, that became some of the very first states of an independent nation.

All of which raises the question of just how much these diminutive New England states are self-conscious about their size. After all, we live in a culture that routinely celebrates big over small. Agree or disagree, the phrase is not, "Size doesn't matter." Try finding a *small* box store.

But I look at it differently in New England. Small is the region's signature, its strength, and a key to its enduring identity. New England isn't home to the world's longest bar (Put-in-Bay, Ohio), the largest highway interchange (Houston, Texas), or the biggest state (Alaska). New England is, in fact, home to the very smallest state of all. (Which, ironically, has the longest official name: "State of Rhode Island and Providence Plantations.")

To my mind, New Englanders over time have responded to their small physical *footprint* by being big thinkers and doing big *things,* seemingly out of proportion to

BRIDGE TO SOMEWHERE

Boston's shortest bridge was designed by William G. Preston in 1867. Tiny, picturesque, and for pedestrians only, it crosses over the narrowest part of the Public Garden's lagoon, itself famous for being home to Swan Boats and wayward ducklings. It's often referred to as the world's smallest suspension bridge, and for a long time it was. But following improvements in 1921, it was technically reclassified as a girder, not a suspension bridge. Technicalities aside, it's still a wicked small bridge.

Suspension Bridge, Boston Public Garden Photo by James A. Barrett/cluelessinboston.com

that size. New England has produced founding fathers, famed inventors, US presidents, authors, artists, orchestras, and world-renowned hospitals and universities. Still, we sure do have a way with small. I mean, anyone can build the biggest suspension bridge. It takes imagination (and a bit of whimsy) to build the smallest.

Little Rhody: Who You Callin' Small?

The state of Rhode Island would fit into Texas about 257 times. Didn't know that, did you? Neither did I. But it's funny what you find out while researching a story about the world of small things in New England. Thus armed with the above intriguing but otherwise useless factoid, I ran it by Denise Kenney, then-editor of the *Warren Times-Gazette* (published continuously since 1866). We had our reasons for dropping in. Warren, Rhode Island, is the smallest town in the smallest county in the smallest state in America.

Warren, Rhode Island Photo by Dave Cleaveland, Maine Imaging

"We like us just the way we are, thank you," says Kenney, who, it turns out, has heard it all before. She wasn't having any of this "smallest" stuff.

Which, in variations, is a sentiment I've heard echoed all around the tiny Ocean State. What Rhode Islanders may lack in square miles, they more than make up for in self-confidence.

Take Buddy Cianci, the former (and longest-serving) mayor of Providence. Cianci's long and colorful political career might very well have gone on forever had it not been abbreviated in 2002 by a federal prison sentence for racketeering conspiracy. (He was released in 2007, wrote a book, and now hosts a popular Rhode Island radio show.) A diminutive but dogged doer, Buddy Cianci is, in some ways, the perfectly imperfect poster child for his state. (After all, in its early days, the state was often referred to derisively as "Rogue's Island.") Colorful and tireless (many would add, "shameless"), Cianci consistently made headlines while, among other things, re-routing a river, rejuvenating his downtown, and marketing his own marinara sauce. He also made headlines by whacking a guy over the head with an ashtray. That last incident did result in a temporary career hiccup. Amazingly though, Cianci regrouped, and was reelected two more times, once unopposed. Go figure.

Napoleon complex? Not in Narragansett. Or Cranston, or Warwick, or Woonsocket. The stuffed quahog—a small and lowly bivalve—is the state's signature food specialty. You gotta problem with that?

They're certainly not sensitive about size in Warren, where they might somehow be expected to be. In fact, at the *Warren Times-Gazette,* Denise Kenney's successor, Ted Hays, adds on a couple of additional (wafer-thin) layers when it comes to their tiny title.

"I tell people I live in the smallest apartment in the smallest apartment building in the smallest town in the smallest county in the smallest state."

Warren, it would seem, is the geographic equivalent of those little Russian Matroyshka dolls.

Actually, it's a lovely (yes, little) town. Located on Rhode Island's East Bay between Newport and Providence, Warren still has a working waterfront, a pretty tree-lined Main Street full of (yes, small) shops and antiques stores.

"Warren is a town that's steeped in tradition," Denise Kenney says, waving to a friend driving by. "I think most people here just think of us as old New England and new. We're a little bit of both, we're right in the middle, and we're not self-conscious, and we're pretty proud."

"And proud of being smallest of the small?"

"You know, I'll bet you there are some people in Warren who don't even realize we're the smallest town in the smallest county in the smallest state," Kenney says.

"Maybe it's better that way."

"I think so," she says.

From Warren, we head back across the bay and about an hour or so south-west to Exeter, Rhode Island. You can't drive far in Rhode Island without see-ing the water. In fact, 17 percent of Rhode Island is water, making it the most water-covered state in America. How generally flat and close to sea level is Rhode Island? The central *landfill* in Johnston is among the state's highest points. Offi-cially, the state's highest point is Jerimoth Hill in Foster, which rises to barely

Yawgoo Valley ski area, Exeter, Rhode Island Photo by Katie Chamberlin

eight hundred feet. So one thing you wouldn't expect to find much of in Rhode Island is skiing. And you won't. Except in Exeter. Where you'll find Yawgoo Valley, Rhode Island's only ski area, and . . . wait for it . . . one of the smallest ski hills in New England.

Over the years, I've skied most of the major ski areas in all six New England states, including a memorable Memorial Day hike up New England's highest peak, Mount Washington, for a steep run down its legendary Tuckerman's Ravine. But on a brisk and sunny late-February morning, we spent a delightful time at little Yawgoo. In truth, most of it was spent not skiing, but chatting at the "base" with feisty and funny Patty DeWardener, who runs Yawgoo with her husband. DeWardener was in a particularly upbeat mood on this day, mostly on account of the four-plus inches of new snow that had fallen overnight.

"Hey, we're here today, we're open, and we're white—for the moment!"

No high-speed quads or sprawling, slope-side condos here. As it has for fifty years, a small and simple lodge looks out at two aging double chairlifts grinding away alongside an even rarer throwback—an old-fashioned New England rope tow. Local kids gather into ski school groups, while senior skiers trudge onto the lifts. There are no lines.

DeWardener and I look up at the hill.

"Do you refer to that as the 'summit' up there?" I ask.

"'Summit,' 'top,' whatever you want to call it, if we're running a lift up to it, we're happy," she says.

"Official elevation?"

"Two hundred forty-five feet," she says. "Longest trail is about a half-mile—*if* snow is made all the way down. Other trails . . . well, if you really zig-zag, you can turn them into half a mile, too," she says coyly.

I press DeWardener about a persistent rumor I'd heard—that the state's central landfill is actually higher than its only ski area.

"Well," she grimaces. "The landfill might have the advantage."

But I'd done some checking, and I had good news.

"Actually, you're eighty-five feet higher."

"That's today," she quickly cautioned. "Unlike us, their hill grows."

Big Green Mountains, Really Small Capital

While Rhode Island is the nation's smallest state, Vermont has its own diminutive distinction: Its capital city, Montpelier, is the smallest state capital in America.

"It's, um, very intimate."

That's how (now former) Governor Jim Douglas describes Montpelier, Vermont, whose population size (around eight thousand) ranks it fiftieth out of fifty state capitals.

"We have two streets here, State and Main. We're on State."

The governor is fond of making corny jokes, which surprises a bit, since his otherwise serious, white-haired, bespectacled and buttoned-down demeanor suggests more accountant than comedian. But he's just getting warmed up. Eyebrows raised, he points a long finger for additional emphasis.

Montpelier Main Street Photo by Jeb Wallace-Brodeur

State House, Montpelier, Vermont Photo by Jeb Wallace-Brodeur

"It's also the only state capital without a McDonald's," he says with more pride than envy.

For a state capital, Montpelier still maintains a genuinely charming small-town vibe, and is as compact as its state house. You can do a full walking circuit of the entire city in less than thirty minutes. That's counting a gaze at the Winooski River from a bridge or two.

"In a way, it's a nine-to-five town," Douglas observes as we stand chatting on the greensward of the state house on a brilliantly blue and clear late-spring afternoon.

"I drive fifty miles from Middlebury every day—Vermont's one of four states without an official governor's residence—so it's a very small city, a real community where people get to know each other."

That they do. In fact, what's always struck me about this seat of Vermont's state government is not the lack of fast food, but the lack of any pomp or pretense when it comes to the politicians here. We'd been standing on the grass down below the state house as we watch Douglas (accompanied by a single aide) make his way down the steps and outside to meet us. And true to form, he is stopped twice, and chats amiably each time. (The second by a young man playing Frisbee. Shirtless. With his dog. Very Vermont.)

"That's typical," Douglas smiles when I remark about the impromptu "Ask the Governor" sessions on his way out the door. "We're a small state, we know each other, and most of us here pride ourselves on being accessible."

Not that state legislators in Montpelier have much choice. Truthfully, there are city halls—even town halls—bigger than Vermont's state house. Stand on State and gaze up at the handsome but simple granite building with the gold dome and you will undoubtedly think, "Wow, that is one really small state house." It used to be even smaller. In the 1850s, after a fire, it was renovated and the two wings were each enlarged by one window bay. (If you look closely at the base of the pillars, you can still see the area darkened by fire.) And while some state officials, including the governor, have offices in another building, the state house's small size means that most Vermont state legislators have no individual offices, giving voters there unusually open access to their representatives. Which they've come to expect. Also very Vermont.

"Vermonters walk into the state house anytime, walk into a committee room, sit down, listen—there aren't any barriers between them and their representatives," says former Vermont House Speaker Gaye Symington. Born in Massachusetts,

Symington became only the second female Speaker of the Vermont House. As Speaker, she did have an office, and a single staff member. "There's a lot less formal appointments, and people are always getting me on the run," Symington laughs. "It means that everyone uses communal spaces to talk, meet with constituents—it creates very direct, retail democracy."

I can attest to that.

Some years earlier, on a different story, we were passing through Montpelier on a blustery winter day. Having never been inside the state house but curious, I wandered over and went inside. The legislature was not in session, there were few people about, and the building was almost eerily quiet. I walked past the formal portraits of former governors and headed up the marble staircase. Passing the "Office of the Governor" doorway, which happened to be open, I stuck my head inside. No one. Well, someone. An older guy was at the copy machine in the corner. I turned to leave.

"Can I help you?"

It was Governor Howard Dean.

I told him I was just visiting, having a look about the building.

"Enjoy," he said.

And he went back to making copies. Two years later he was running for president.

"Very Howard," laughed Dean's successor, Jim Douglas, who proceeded to share a final, small oddity about Vermont's state house.

"It's the only one in America whose dome has no rotunda below it."

In other words, Montpelier's gold dome is actually a big, gleaming hood ornament—all cosmetic effect, with no practical purpose.

Sure enough, with the help of a maintenance worker, my photographer, Carl, and I climb a series of stairs and ladders to what seems like an attic. Under a huge, curving cupola. The dome.

"It's all gold and nice and everything from the outside," Gaye Symington says of the dome. "But inside, let's face it—it's really just a Vermont silo."

The governor, however, clearly prefers to see the value of a faux dome over a full rotunda.

"I think it's an example of the thrift of Vermonters," argues Jim Douglas. "We don't like all that empty space."

Really, who needs it?

Mr. Morrill's Miniatures

In this book, I devote a chapter to some of the extraordinarily skilled New England artisans and craftspeople we've met. Winson Morrill is one of those people. But he's not in that chapter. He's in this one. Because what's unique about Win Morrill's craft can only be described by one simple word: small. Well, two words: astonishingly small.

"People say, 'Wow, I don't believe it.' And I'll show 'em some more and the 'Wows' get a little bigger; I guess I get a lot of 'Wows.' Just like you guys did."

He's right. That's exactly how Carl (my photographer) and I reacted.

When we first met Winson Morrill, he was a few months shy of his eighty-seventh birthday. He lives in South Hamilton, Massachusetts, just inland from Boston's north shore. It's an area that has pockets of real, old-time Yankee wealth. Hamilton itself is home to a number of sprawling horse farms, not to mention the famed Myopia Hunt Club. (Think polo and all that goes with it.)

Morrill doesn't live in that part of Hamilton.

Winson Morrill at work Photo courtesy of *Chronicle*/WCVB-TV

He was a greenhouse grower in nearby (and more working-class) Peabody for forty-five years. He lives now on a fixed income in a tiny, one-story wood-frame house down a narrow little dirt road off a slightly larger street. He's tucked away. He even seems tucked away within his own little living room when we enter. It's tough getting up, tough moving around, even tough to see on this day; he's had some kind of eye infection and his squint is as prominent as his warm smile.

"Please, sit," I insist.

It's easy enough for Carl and me to get the grand tour on our own; there are only three small rooms. I lean in to the kitchen to put my jacket on a chair. The fridge is covered with photos of Winson Morrill's two grandchildren at various ages, and his one daughter, their mom. His wife, Jean, died in 2003.

It's no use asking Win Morrill to sit. His work literally rings the tiny place, covering every inch of shelf and assorted small tables, and he wants to lead us, point things out, hurriedly tweaking and rearranging a piece here and there. Even as frail and unsteady as he is, even with a red and swollen eye, Morrill is beaming as he watches us take it all in. And he has every right to.

What Winson Morrill makes are spectacularly tiny miniatures: exquisitely detailed miniature rooms lined with even smaller bookshelves . . . which are lined with still-tinier books the size of a thumbnail . . . all of which have real bindings that open up to real paper pages that have actual writing on them. I look at them, and look back at Win, my mouth open. These are miniatures that, in their almost microscopic detail, seem to defy the fact that they've all been made by hand. One hand. When he was seven, Morrill contracted infantile paralysis—polio—in the epidemic of 1931. Only one arm and hand function normally.

Not that he wants to talk about it much.

"Wasn't just me, was a lot of poor kids back then," he exhales as he eases himself back into his armchair. "I could never lift my arm after that, but fortunately for me, the fingers were okay, so all the work I did growing flowers, I'd pick up my polio hand with my other arm and I could use the fingers like this. . . ."

He never sells his work, but does enjoy giving them as gifts. He gave a ship in a bottle to the actress Rita Moreno, after they'd met when Winson appeared on the TV show *What's My Line?* in 1974. He made his first miniature book for his grandson, and has since churned out over ten thousand of them, along with the equally miniature shelves and rooms to display them all in.

"I never make one at a time," he says. "I find some antique paper that I like, and make probably ten at a time."

Books on a penny, dime Photo courtesy of *Chronicle*/WCVB-TV

Ten at a time, each one going through the same laborious process involving cutting, clamping, soaking, binding, gluing, and trimming. All hunched over a lamp at a cluttered kitchen table, all to make a stamp-size book, and on to the next one.

"Books always fascinated me," he says softly, slowly rubbing his closed eyes. "I only went as far as the tenth grade, but I've always been interested in reading. All the books you see in the miniature libraries have titles. A lot of 'em are books I've read."

I lean over toward a miniature furnished study, and gently pry a book the size of my thumb nail from a shelf shorter than my little finger. Sure enough, the cover reads, *Tobacco Road.*

"Open the drawer on that little table under the shelf," Win says mischievously. "You might want to use the magnifying glass." He has several all around his pieces, for just this purpose.

The tiny drawer opens to reveal an even tinier inlaid bit of photograph, a sepia-colored piece of family history, faded but real. These whimsical "secrets" are built in to all of Morrill's miniature rooms. Carpets reveal hidden floors underneath, walls conceal secret closets with yet more tiny, hidden finds within. There's something very Alice-in-Wonderland about it all.

"That's become the real fun part for me, those little secrets," he grins like a kid. "You'd never know they were there unless I showed them to you."

I look at my watch. It's nearly noon, and we've somehow been in this small living room surrounded by this small world for more than two hours. Morrill jokes that his day is almost over.

"I'm in bed every day at six-thirty, by hook or by crook, no matter what."

He's up at three o'clock in the morning, has a quick breakfast, then goes on the computer, which he bought a few years back, to tend to his Facebook page. Then it's back to his miniatures.

"The idea my daughter and I had was to get all my work on the computer, and show it off in a dignified way. And I've done that."

I ask him about what he thinks or hopes will happen to all his work.

"I'd like to give things away to some museums or historical societies. I heard on the computer from someone I gave a ship-in-a-bottle to maybe thirty or forty years ago; they still have it and sent me a picture of it. That makes me feel good, to think of my name on it, that it will always be there, and someone appreciates it."

He's quiet for a few moments. We sit. I hear the kitchen clock ticking.

"I know my daughter and my grandkids are very proud of me. That's a legacy, too."

Carl and I gather up our coats and prepare to leave. Grabbing my outstretched arm, and with effort, Winson Morrill gets himself standing again. He tells us he's going to get back to work after we leave; he'd seen a few things earlier that "could use a little tinkering."

I tell him it's been a pleasure and a privilege to see his work. He pats my hand, and looks over at his shelves.

"I guess maybe I was always trying to prove that with my handicap, I was equally as good as anyone else."

I'd say he succeeded.

BELLY UP TO THE (VERY SMALL) BAR

Needless to say, Boston has its share of Irish pubs and taverns. Some of them are small and cozy. But only one is officially called The Littlest Bar. For over half a century, The Littlest stood—more squatted, just below street level—on the equally tiny Providence Street, a short jog just past Old City Hall. How small was The Littlest at its littlest? Most conference rooms are larger. Full (legal) capacity was about thirty-eight people, not including bar staff. When ice was needed, patrons gladly formed a human assembly line to pass it from the machine to the bar.

"You really got to know people here, that's for sure," says Littlest owner Paddy Grace.

Alas, in 2006, a condo development forced The Littlest from its tiny perch on Providence. Grace has since moved the bar to somewhat roomier quarters (think two conference rooms) on Broad Street near the waterfront. It's in a historic old stone building, has a lovely feel, and the Guinness is drawn as expertly as ever. It's just not quite as small as it once was.

"God bless our customers" says Grace. "A lot of them have followed us over here, and we make new friends all the time."

Still, you can rest assured that The Littlest Bar is that rare establishment *not* bragging about being bigger.

The new, slightly bigger, Littlest Bar

Harbor Colors, Rockport, Massachusetts Photo by Mark Kanegis

CHAPTER 3

THE PLACES

California covers over 163,000 square miles. By contrast, all six New England states together make up just under 72,000. Yet within that area is a remarkable range of dramatic physical contrasts, from six-thousand-foot, above-tree-line mountains and alpine meadows, to sea-level surf, sand, and tidal estuaries, all separated by a mere three hours or so of driving. Thirty minutes from downtown Boston, there are working farms and working waterfronts, woods, and wide open areas. Thoreau was enraptured by the stillness of Walden Pond, by idylls on the Concord River, and sojourns to Cape Cod and the Maine woods. For good reason. By contrast, other writers and artists have focused, often poignantly, on the urban places where New Englanders have long worked and played and struggled, in mill cities like Manchester, Lawrence, Lowell, and Fall River, and in historic waterfront cities like Portland, Portsmouth, Gloucester, New Bedford, and Boston.

In my travels, I've been in and around and impressed by all of these places. Some places that follow are well known; others are more off the beaten path. Some are places we've returned to many times; some left a lasting impression with a single visit. What follows is certainly not a comprehensive list, nor a tourist guide. They're simply places whose stories, for a variety of reasons, have stayed with me. And which, in their own way, illustrate something essential about New England.

He Lives Yet

Notches are to New England what "passes," "gaps," and "cols" are to other regions of America. New Hampshire alone has over thirty-five notches, and several—like Crawford, Franconia, and Pinkham—are as draped with colorful history and grandeur as the jagged peaks that rise above them. Indeed, Pinkham Notch is home to the northeast's highest point: 6,288-foot Mount Washington. The deep greens and purples of Franconia inspired Robert Frost as he sat on the small porch of his home in nearby Sugar Hill. In Crawford Notch, a railroad snakes intrepidly up through steep and seemingly impenetrable walls of granite. (To ride it over the famed Frankenstein Trestle, appearing to be suspended in mid-air for three minutes, is an unforgettable high—literally.)

But in Franconia Notch there was an unrivaled something else: an Old Man to watch over it. And to look up to. Formed by the glaciers and perched high on a mountainside above the notch, it offered those passing through a singular, if fleeting thrill—a glimpse of New England's most famous profile. Native American legends referred to it simply as "The Great Stone Face," and it surely was: the craggy, granite, yet unmistakable visage of a man—massive forehead, beak-like nose, sharp, jutting chin—peering out proudly, silently, to the east.

Part of the lure in driving by was the sheer anticipation; it took several minutes for the actual payoff view. Composed of several, overlapping ledges of rock, the great, granite "face" was really something of an illusion. On the approach, you

The Great Stone Face: The Old Man of the Mountain, Franconia Notch, New Hampshire Photo courtesy of Old Man of the Mountain Legacy Fund

knew you were looking up at the right place on the cliffs, but saw just a jumble of rock. Only on rounding a curve just past Profile Lake did it all come together in an instant: the huge, overhanging slabs suddenly all lining up visually like an immense aerial Rubik's Cube. And for five seconds or so, there he was.

The Old Man of the Mountain was the state symbol and a source of deep and enduring pride for generations of New Hampshire natives, like Daniel Webster, who famously wrote, "Men hang out their signs indicative of their respective trades; shoe makers hang out a gigantic shoe; jewelers a monster watch, and the dentist hangs out a gold tooth; but up in the Mountains of New Hampshire, God Almighty has hung out a sign to show that there, He makes men."

"I looked up and saluted him every night," says Dick Hamilton, a spry, white-haired Granite-Stater in his seventies with a quick smile, deep-lined face and deeper, folksy laugh. Hamilton, a North Conway native, was president of White Mountain Attractions for thirty-five years, an organization which promoted that area of New Hampshire.

Dick Hamilton, Franconia Notch, New Hampshire
Photo courtesy of *Chronicle*/WCVB-TV

"He was my boss," Hamilton is fond of saying. "He was the state's number one attraction—four to six million people saw him every year, and every night on my way back up to Littleton from Lincoln, I would look up at him and say, 'Goodnight, Boss.'"

And then, incredibly, this glacial relic of the last Ice Age, this landmark through the millennia whose likeness adorned everything from coins to highway signs to license plates . . . was no longer there to say goodnight to.

In the end, there was little mystery. The year 2003 saw a stubborn spring in the notoriously weather-changing White Mountains of New Hampshire. May began with several days of raw, steady rain. Up on Cannon Mountain, water was driven deeply and relentlessly into the cracks and crevices of the ledges comprising the Old Man's profile. Then, on the night of May 3, temperatures in these higher elevations dropped steadily. In those cracks, water turned to ice and expanded.

"We think it began with the stone that formed his Adam's apple, which was the center of weight balance for the Old Man," surmises Hamilton. "And when that went, the weight shifted forward, and all five ledges, which were already pitched slightly forward, well. . . ."

Two campers, asleep in their van on the valley floor, later said they heard a low rumble in the night, which they thought was thunder. It wasn't. What they heard was the Old Man of the Mountain's thunderous, rocky death rattle. In a matter of seconds, what had held for twelve thousand years fell twelve hundred feet, and into pieces. He was gone.

"I was sound asleep and got a phone call from an employee of mine about seven-thirty," says Dick Hamilton. "She said, 'The Old Man's fallen.' I said, 'What??' She said, 'The Old Man's fallen.' I made it from Littleton to the Old Man faster than you want to know, pulled into the northbound parking lot, looked up, and did this. . . ."

Hamilton's hand comes up over his mouth, his eyes wide as he looks up at where the Old Man was. We're standing below the Cannon Mountain cliffs on a sunny October day, four years after the morning he's describing. But he's back in the shock of that moment. Slowly, the hand comes down, but he's still looking up at the cliffs.

"I couldn't believe it," he says softly, shaking his head. "I really could not believe it."

Hamilton wasn't alone in his emotional reaction. The Old Man's fall was front page news around the world. The state of New Hampshire received over three thousand notes and messages of condolence. At the site itself, visitors left flowers at the base of the cliff, as if a living person had perished.

For Dave Nielsen, it felt exactly like that. He and his late dad were closer to the Old Man than anyone. Literally. After Niels Nielsen passed away in 2001, some of his ashes were placed in the Old Man's left eye. It seemed fitting. In 1965, Nielsen was appointed the first official caretaker of the Old Man, a role he passed on to his son in 1991. For forty years, the pair made three trips a year up to the Old Man, maintenance missions full of physical gutsiness and genuine risk, as they rappelled out over the great rock face to care for their unique charge.

In the mid-60s, a famous Associated Press photo ran on front pages all over the world. It showed a harnessed Niels Nielsen, dangling out over the Old Man's face, snipping away weeds. "Nose Job," read the caption.

Fall 2005: Gone Photo courtesy of Old Man of the Mountain Legacy Fund

"My dad used to talk to the Old Man when he went out over the edge," Dave Nielsen recalls. "He'd pat him and say, 'Okay, I won't pinch if you won't sneeze.' You'd get into a particular position up there and just talk to him like he was a human being, and you began to share things; he really became part of our family, like a grandfather or a favorite uncle."

But those closest to the Old Man, like Dick Hamilton and the Nielsens, also understood a tough truth that most of the public didn't fully appreciate.

"We knew he'd come down someday; we just didn't think it would be in our lifetime," Hamilton acknowledges. "We were trying to save it for our grandchildren and great-grandchildren—that's why all that work was being done up there, to try and seal the cracks."

Indeed, what the casual observer on the ground didn't see were the huge, protruding turnbuckles and steel tie-rods, the waterproof canopies and special concrete calking, all installed within the past century to try to anchor and stabilize those five huge, separate, and vulnerable rock slabs that together formed the famous face. It was a noble, hard-fought battle. But the outcome, alas, had been preordained by nature.

"I promoted him most of my professional life," says Dick Hamilton, running a hand slowly through a head of thick, wavy, gray hair. "And it wasn't long after he was gone that I thought, well, maybe I should be, too. And I retired."

Today, it might seem as if all that sad remembrance would simply hang over Franconia Notch like a mournful and ghostly fog. Not that the Old Man isn't missed. He is, terribly. But the story of his fall involves more than epitaph. There's also an epilogue. And it's called for Dick Hamilton to put his promoter hat on again.

In the wake of the Old Man's demise, all sorts of ideas were floated for what to do at the site. Some ideas (build a replica) were easily dismissed; others (reassemble him) were more appealing but no less unrealistic.

"My immediate feeling was to do nothing," Hamilton says flatly. "The Good Lord put him up there, and nature decided it was time for him to go."

Across the state, however, a powerful desire to memorialize the Old Man emerged. The Old Man of the Mountain Legacy Fund was established to spearhead a national competition for proposals from artists. Dick Hamilton became chairman. Private funds were raised, and proposals poured in. Eventually, thirty-one sculptors were considered. But according to Hamilton, the final choice was not a difficult one.

"We said, 'Oh, my God—that's it.' We just knew."

It's hard to convey just how brilliantly and simply Massachusetts sculptors Ron Magers and Shelly Bradbury chose to memorialize the Old Man of the Mountain. There is no statue or likeness, per se. Instead, there's an ingenious opportunity to recreate the actual *experience* of what it was like to view him.

"My feeling was, let's create something where you get in touch with your inner child," Ron Magers explains, sitting on a rock by the lake. "That's what the Old Man brought out for everyone that viewed him—you had to get yourself in just the right place and the right position to bring all those stones together to create that magnificent face of his."

Magers, who also designs toys, seems to have channeled his own inner-toymaker in creating his "pro-filers." Facing up at the cliff, they've been best described as looking like upside-down hockey sticks. In the air, at the end of the pole, is an arm made up of a series of small sculpted pieces—each a perfect miniature match of the various outcroppings that made up the Old Man's pro-file. And as you adjust your view at the profiler, placing the gathering image up at the cliff just right . . . he is there again.

Profiler, Old Man of
the Mountain Memorial
Photo by Ron Magers

"Sure, it's a little trickery of the eye," Magers concedes. "We're not putting the Old Man back up there, but in one magical, little way, we are."

And that's the creative genius of what Magers and Bradbury have done.

The seven profilers have been installed; a dedication ceremony was held at the memorial site on June 12, 2011. For her part, Shelly Bradbury chose to create on a far bigger scale. (Which has meant bigger fundraising before it's finished.)

"I wanted it to have an ancient, mysterious feel, almost like the idea of Stonehenge," Bradbury says. "To walk, around it, touch it, and be a little bit in awe."

Her sculpture will sit at the end of a long path leading down to Profile Lake. Five twenty-foot granite slabs will, like the Old Man, collectively reveal the famous profile.

"What I love about it," Bradbury says with relish, "is that by themselves, these large stones mean nothing, they're abstract; but at the right perspective, these meaningless pieces of granite become something and have meaning again."

Below the cliffs today, the lake no longer reflects the very thing for which it's named. But it's still Profile Lake. In Franconia Notch, something powerful still endures. If only in memory.

"It's pretty unusual," Dick Hamilton says wryly. "A bunch of rocks fall down, and you remember. Because you saw it, and it made an impression on you."

And somehow, it still does.

The Other Cape: Cape Ann

When someone in New England refers to "the Cape," it's understood what that means. But Cape Cod is not the state's only cape. It's just the bigger and more famous one.

"We like it that way," laughs Mark Kanegis. "We don't mind that more people go to Cape Cod than Cape Ann."

A Rockport native in his forties, Kanegis is a talented landscape photographer who owns a gallery on the town's Bearskin Neck, a popular row of shops and artist galleries extending out into Rockport Harbor.

"I mean, those of us who own businesses, we don't mind people coming, but that's one of the things that makes Cape Ann unique and special—it's *not* Cape Cod."

No, it's not. And fewer tourists, traffic, and minigolf courses is only part of it.

Jutting out into the Atlantic about thirty miles northeast of Boston, Cape Ann forms the upper lip of Massachusetts Bay. (Cape Cod to the south forms the lower one.) You can drive directly onto Cape Ann and reach historic Ipswich, but to reach the easternmost-end of the Cape, you'll eventually need to cross the A. Piatt Andrew Bridge over the Annisquam River. The bridge wasn't built until the late 1940s, and many residents, long used to life a little bit apart, lamented being more connected with the mainland. Today, that perhaps unconscious island mindset of independence and creativity still best characterizes the tip of Cape Ann, and the two unique communities that comprise it, Gloucester and Rockport.

Besides Cape Ann's Native American inhabitants, Europeans had established thriving seasonal fishing settlements there long before the Pilgrims arrived off Cape Cod in 1620. By 1623, Gloucester was already a permanent fishing village. Today, while working boats from Maine to Rhode Island continue to fan out to the great Atlantic fishing grounds, it's Gloucester alone whose name is synonymous with the history of fishing in America.

It's a history, particularly in the modern era, that's had more ups and downs than a heaving sea. The famed fisherman on Gloucester's iconic statue stands forever steadfast at a ship's wheel, above the poetic words from the 107th psalm: "*They that go down to the sea in Ships . . .*" Below that, in starker prose, are inscribed

Gloucester Harbor Photo by Mark Kanegis

the names of some of the thousands of Gloucestermen who've gone down to that very sea and never returned (like the crew of the *Andrea Gail,* the trawler lost in 1991 and made famous in the book and subsequent film, *The Perfect Storm*). But nature hasn't thinned the fishing ranks here all by itself. In recent years, the combined forces of a lousy economy, overfishing, and crushing federal regulations have together buffeted New England's fishery like a man-made perfect storm of its own, ultimately sweeping more boats off the water than Mother Nature ever could.

"It used to be three or four boats abreast all up and down every dock here; now you can see how it's atrophied."

Scott Swicker is tying up his day boat, *Aaron & Alexa,* on a bright, brisk spring morning. Offshore gusts turn up a chop even in the protected enclave of Gloucester's inner harbor.

Gloucester Fisherman's Memorial Photo by Kirk Kittell

"Still, I love what I do," says Swicker matter-of-factly. "The people that are left here have it in their blood, getting up every day, watching the sun rise, knowing every day's a different challenge."

Swicker's a dark-haired, rugged-looking, straight-talking, middle-aged Gloucester native who's been fishing for more than thirty years. In a way, he's the face of both his profession and his city today: tired and toughened, but determined to adapt, to hang in and hang on, as steadfastly as the fisherman portrayed in that statue. Gloucester is not San Francisco's Fisherman's Wharf or Manhattan's South Street Seaport. It's the original—America's most authentic, enduring, working waterfront. Sure it's changed, but the magnificent harbor here is the reason fishermen have clung tenaciously to this spot for nearly five hundred years.

We're at the dock to meet Swicker as he guides his boat in. Generally, he and his crew are up at three in the morning, out to the fishing grounds by daylight, putting in twelve tough hours of work on the water before returning to offload a catch that might include cod, haddock, or yellow-tail flounder. But this day's been a short one. Swicker's been fishing Stellwagen Bank, a huge offshore marine

Scott Swicker, Skipper of the *Aaron & Alexa*, Gloucester, Massachusetts
Photo courtesy of *Chronicle*/WCVB-TV

sanctuary between Cape Ann and Cape Cod. He'd like to fish Jeffrey's Ledge, but it's closed off until July due to fish spawning. The government calls them "rolling closures." Frustrated fishermen have other words for the welter of complex and frequently changing federal regulations they're forced to follow. But the fines can be swift and steep, so Swicker's settled for simply targeting his codfish limit and heading back in. Way it is nowadays.

"The regs have definitely made life a lot more difficult," Swicker says, rubbing his eyes. "Definitely the age of fishermen has changed. I'm about the average age, and when I started there were a lot of young guys going into it. Now we're growing up, getting older, but you don't see many young guys getting into it these days."

Indeed, the slow but relentless decrease in maritime activity on Gloucester's waterfront has created vacant space along the curving harbor's half-moon, like unsightly gaps in what was once a full and cocky, confident smile. For years now, the city has had to do some soul-searching, as it struggles over how best to integrate new elements into its former, fishing-only identity. In other words, what else can this place be?

"It's always been a fishing community, it's been a fishing community for almost four hundred years, and it's going to be a fishing community," says Richard Gaines, a gruff but well-respected longtime reporter for the *Gloucester Times,* who's covered the city's waterfront struggles for years.

"But fishing's not going to be a big enough part of the economy in the future, so it has to reinvent itself as something else along with fishing."

It's that elusive and hotly debated "something else" that continues to animate the conversation about Gloucester's waterfront. There are strict and sometimes frustrating state mandates regarding maritime use. There are longstanding tensions between those who welcome new development, and traditionalists who fear that each vanished fishing boat or business brings the waterfront one condo closer to becoming "Newport North." But slowly, things evolve. A cruise terminal has opened, creating optimism that a new, non-fishing business can indeed help rejuvenate the waterfront. Other mixed-use development plans are slowly taking shape as well. On Main Street, new shops and restaurants brim with life. There is a thriving and exciting local music scene, and increasing numbers of professionals who work in Boston and elsewhere are finding an appeal in the city's scrappy but spirited sense of community. The fishermen who've remained for the most part retain a guarded optimism that the trimmed-down fleet is facing an improving future.

"Gloucester has never taken the easy way out," says Gaines. "It has turned away from opportunities to become a nouveau kind of city, and it's paid a price for that; we're at least at a starting point for a redefinition of Gloucester."

Not all of Gloucester needs redefining. Nor is its fishing community the only one of legend. On Rocky Neck, one of America's oldest art colonies still thrives.

"People would be surprised to know how many really significant artists spent summers here," observes Gordon Goettemann. "Winslow Homer was here, Edward Hopper was here—I mean, you can't open a book on American art history of the late nineteenth century and not see examples of artists who made work in Gloucester."

A Midwesterner, Goettemann and his wife, Judy (an equally talented painter), have returned here every summer for over forty years to paint and run the gallery they own on the Neck. They've seen changes in the art colony; what's remained unchanged, though, is their favorite subject to paint on Cape Ann: its famous light.

"I'm not going to try and explain it from a physical standpoint," Goettemann tells me, sitting on a wooden bench in front of his Rocky Neck gallery. "But I can tell you it's phenomenal, and by that I mean there are occasions when it is so exceptionally unique and beautiful that it takes your breath away."

Mark Kanegis, sitting in his own gallery down the road a few miles in Rockport, agrees.

Twin Lights, Thatcher Island, Cape Ann, Massachusetts Photo by Mark Kanegis

"I grew up in Rockport, I've traveled a lot, and every time I still feel like I can't wait to get back here to take pictures."

It's understandable. Each bend on winding Route 27 opens up new angles on the ocean beside it . . . a different light, a change in color, a different view of the water. One of my favorite spots at a big bend in that road in Rockport is a largely hidden gem named Halibut Point. It's a state park that's the site of a former granite quarry, and a World War II coastal observation tower. (It also happens to be the closest spot in the continental United States to the continent of Europe.) Along the shore, you can walk amongst huge rocks just up from a crashing surf, and find protected perches and nooks and crannies in which to sit and just look out at the ocean. It's the sort of place where hours seem to pass like minutes.

Mark Kanegis gets that.

Lobsterman Gussie Contrino Photo by Mark Kanegis

"There's a lot of good karma here when I go out to shoot," he says. "As long as it's not pouring rain, you're always bound to find something interesting to paint or photograph; that's the nature of Cape Ann, it's the nature of Rockport."

In his gallery, I admire some of the framed color prints on the wall: a line of fishing boats in Gloucester Harbor; the power of a storm-churned surf; a grinning lobsterman hauling up traps on a glassy-calm Pigeon Cove.

"That's Gussie," Mark grins.

An hour later, alongside Rockport's T-Wharf, we're talking with Gussie Contrino himself.

"I love this place, it's the town I grew up in," he says, arms wide to take it all in. "And I'm proud to be a fisherman—it's what I wanted to do since I was a wee lad."

Motif #1 (and #2), Rockport Harbor, Cape Ann, Masschusetts Photo by Mark Kanegis

Looking out in the harbor, Gussie and I joke about the town's most famous structure, the bright red, former fishing shack turned permanent painting/photo subject known universally as Motif #1. For the first time, I notice the smaller, gray building directly behind it.

"That's 'Motif #2,'" Gussie says.

"Funny, that doesn't really show up in the guidebooks does it?"

"Just between the old timers," he winks.

Over the years, Mark Kanegis and Gussie Contrino have become good friends. Kanegis has photographed Gussie many times as he's worked away on the stern of *Gussie's Girls*.

"We get along well," Kanegis says of what he describes today as a roughly "fifty-fifty" mix between the artists and the remaining combination of fishermen and lobstermen. Both communities have deep roots along the rocky shore of this Cape Ann town. The fishermen have baited up here for hundreds of years, and the art colony calls itself the nation's oldest.

"By now we coexist like an old couple," Kanegis laughs. "I think there are days when the artists who're cooped up in the galleries wish they were on the boats, and there are certainly days when the waves are big and the fishermen wish they were in the galleries, so occasionally there's some jealousy, but you know, it works out pretty well."

That same sentiment seems to sum up Cape Ann's unique overall identity: a rich and shared history of fishermen and artists, now as deep and ingrained as the granite on which this spit of land itself sits.

Back at the dock, Scott Swicker has unloaded his catch, dismissed his crew, and is headed home to see his family, have a decent dinner, and get some sleep. Tomorrow, like everyone else on Cape Ann, he'll be at it again.

"Hey, I'm not going to call it 'biblical,' or anything," Swicker laughs. "But you feel like you're part of this long tradition here, you know?"

And with that, he's into his truck, another chapter of tradition in the books.

A Wonder in Woonsocket: "America's Sistine Chapel"

I've always been amused at the wide variety of ways that potential stories have crossed my radar. Only one, though, has come about as a direct result of coaching my older daughter's softball team. Before a practice, the mother of one of her teammates told me about her childhood church in Woonsocket, Rhode Island. She said it had the largest collection of frescoes in North America, and was known as "America's Sistine Chapel." A month later, I was standing inside it, wondering how I could have been unaware of something so spectacular, so close to home.

Woonsocket, Rhode Island, is one of those places in New England that quickly comes to mind when the subject turns to "tired, old, former mill towns." That's not a knock on the city today. "Former," in this case refers to a hundred years ago. (Besides, its oldest radio station, WOON/1240 AM, boasts some of the coolest call letters anywhere.) And Woonsocket's hardly alone in New England in having its industrial heyday long behind it. From Lewiston, Maine, to Manchester, New Hampshire, down through Lawrence, Haverhill, and Fall River, Massachusetts, and on into Pawtucket and Woonsocket, Rhode Island, the nineteenth-century Industrial Revolution made manufacturing powerhouses of these river cities. And when the boom faded a century or so later, it meant another century of struggle for these places—to regroup, re-tool, and reinvent themselves as best they could.

Woonsocket lies on the Blackstone River in northeastern Rhode Island, just over the Massachusetts border. It has a population of just over forty thousand, but once it was larger. The river powered the mills that drew immigrant labor from all over the world during the late nineteenth and early twentieth centuries. By 1900, 60 percent of Woonsocket's population was French-Canadian, and it was considered one of the most French cities in America.

This thriving French-Canadian immigrant community in Woonsocket re-created many of the commercial, social, and religious institutions it had left behind in Quebec. One of these was the Roman Catholic parish of St. Ann's, founded in 1890 to serve the primarily poor French Canadians who'd come to work the mills. As church history has it, the small, modest building was "literally paid for with nickels and dimes." The parish grew, and by 1914, a larger space was needed. Money was again raised, work was begun, and the cathedral-like building that still stands at 84 Cumberland Street was officially opened in the winter of 1918. At a final cost of $150,000, there was little embellishment: Interior walls and ceilings were made entirely of gray stucco cement, and there was no marble or stained glass, nor color of any kind. What was to mark St. Ann's as truly extraordinary wasn't to come for decades.

By the church's thirty-fifth anniversary in 1925, the parish clearly felt a need to add some color to their rather drab building. More funds were raised, and forty-eight stained glass windows were purchased. By the time of the church's fiftieth anniversary in 1940, the appetite for more color inside St. Ann's seems to have grown stronger. According to church history, a search was begun to commission an artist to simply "paint a few paintings to break up the monotony of the gray stucco." They found their artist in Guido Nincheri. But Nincheri had far grander ideas.

He was born and educated in Florence, Italy, and was trained in the artistic style of Michelangelo, Donatello, and Raphael. Nincheri's previous commissions,

Frescoes in St. Ann's, Woonsocket, Rhode Island

however, had not drawn on his real passion—the fresco style that Michelangelo himself had perfected in painting the ceiling of Rome's Sistine Chapel. Ironically, thanks to the shoestring budget that had built St. Ann's, that style was about to be introduced to North America.

"When Nincheri entered the building, the first thing he noticed was that the walls and the ceilings hadn't been plastered—so he was very excited."

So is Dominique Doiron in retelling the story, as we stand on the floor of the church staring up. Nincheri's ceiling is stunning: The scale itself is immense, the colors so rich and vibrant they still pop out even on this overcast day. I'm blown away. Doiron understands.

"You tell people about it, but they only believe it once they step foot in the door," he sighs.

A young and friendly man in his thirties with dark hair, Doiron grew up in St. Ann's Parish. He studies and performs opera, and some of his earliest memories at the church are of hearing his father sing "Ave Maria" on Christmas Eve here.

"Fresco involves painting on a wet plaster surface," Doiron explains. "If the walls here had already been plastered—as they usually are—it would have been impossible."

"In other words," I say, "Nincheri realized he had a rare blank canvas . . ."

"He realized he had more than a blank canvas," Doiron continues. "He had the opportunity to paint in the true fresco style, the same style as Michelangelo's Sistine Chapel."

And on a much bigger canvas, too: The cozy Sistine Chapel would virtually fit inside the cavernous St. Ann's.

There were challenges. Although he was originally contracted for $25,000 in 1940 to finish the project in two years, Nincheri ultimately took eight; the war years made getting supplies difficult. In addition, special scaffolding needed to be constructed. Unlike Michelangelo, Nincheri could not paint up at the ceiling by lying flat. He was a hunchback.

"The scaffolding was built so that it was four or five feet away from the ceiling, and he would sit on a stool or a five-gallon pail and just paint all day long," Doiron explains.

Nincheri was also sensitive to who was paying his contracted bill to paint St. Ann's—its largely working-class parishioners. He rewarded them with a sort of immortality. They became his models.

"These everyday parishioners ended up as angels, apostles, the Virgin Mary." Doiron is drawing his finger in the air across the vast fresco, pointing out individuals, few of whom are still alive.

"Every single face up there is a person who sat in these pews."

In some ways, apart from the stunning achievement of the artwork itself, what's most striking about the frescoes is the simple fact of *where* they are.

"People expect to perhaps find a place like this in Newport or something, but not in Woonsocket," says Doiron quietly. "This was a mill town, a working-class parish, this wasn't a wealthy church."

Today, it's technically not even a church. In October of 2000, as part of a consolidation, the Diocese of Providence closed St. Ann's. Incredibly, there was talk of demolishing it. In an effort to save and preserve the building, a mix of art lovers and former parishioners came together to form the nonprofit St. Ann Arts and Cultural Center. They succeeded. And like its original incarnation, the building is again serving the community, but it's a more diverse one now. There are services on Sunday mornings, a cabaret series, and community theater groups and other organizations are being encouraged to become involved and take ownership as well. And above it all, Guido Nincheri's sprawling frescoes still endure and enrapture. Doiron, who is director of the center, is talking about a long-ago parish, but he could be talking about this new community here as well.

"What's great about this building is that this is proof that when a community works together for a common goal, it can accomplish a lot, and this is what they did—they worked together, they pooled their money, and built for themselves something great."

And then they refused to see it all lost. Imagine that.

Hands Down, Down East

For starters, you have to love a place that is well north of Boston, but is popularly referred to as being "down east" of it. Then there's the accent. You can't easily describe (much less mimic) a true—and truly thick—Maine accent. But it's as much something to savor as a meaty "lobsta" bisque, or a really chunky "chowduh."

Maine is literally out of the way. It's the only American state that borders just one other state (New Hampshire). That's fine with most Mainers, thank you. In Maine, an out-of-stater (like me) is automatically a "flatlander," "from away." Yet despite being New England's largest state, most visitors see only the relative sliver of its spectacular coast, and little of its huge but less accessible interior. Ninety percent of Maine is forested (they don't call it the Pine Tree State for nothing), and vast tracts of land, much of it paper industry–owned, spread out for hundreds of miles away from the ocean. You can drive a long, long way between towns. All of which seems to be of a piece with Maine's rugged, independent profile, and perfectly suits this state that can at times seem a bit taciturn and stand-offish. Old-time Mainers are not an overly talkative bunch; there's a decided tendency to say as little as necessary.

I offer an example from personal experience.

In my early twenties, I spent a summer working on Maine's Mount Desert Island. A friend and I had managed to borrow a coworker's beat-up car for the day, but it broke down on a hilly stretch of road in the little town of Somesville (which is on the shores, by the way, of Somes Sound, the only natural fiord on North America's eastern seaboard). We saw a sign pointing down the road to a gas station, and just beyond the sign, a house with an old fellow sitting on his front porch. We pushed the car as far as the house.

"Hi," I called out to the man. "Is there a mechanic at that gas station up ahead?"

"Yes, sir," he answered in a low, even voice.

"Thank you."

We continued pushing the car down the road. Seconds later, we heard the same low, even voice from the porch behind us.

"Won't find him there today, though."

No, we wouldn't have. We did push the car there, though. And when we met the mechanic the next day, we recognized him immediately, too. Our friend from the porch.

Not that some Mainers can't be coaxed a bit out of their hardy shells. Just ask Peter Mehegan, my former colleague at *Chronicle*.

"Like the Irish, Mainers enjoy chatting with strangers," Mehegan contends. "It's all in the approach."

When it comes to anything Maine, I'd hate to argue with Peter Mehegan. He may technically be a flatlander, but there are more than a few Mainers who'd gladly confer on him some sort of honorary native status. Over nearly thirty years, Pete crafted wonderful stories from virtually every county in Maine, racking up hundreds of thousands of miles in his trademark '68 gold Chevy. His secret to striking up a conversation in Maine?

"All it takes is a few friendly observations about the weather or the state of the lobster fishery to get them started."

Now you try it.

At any rate, your best chance of chatting up a Mainer is along the coast, mostly because a huge majority of the state's 1.3 million people live there. And who can blame them? As the crow (or seagull) flies, Maine's entire coastline measures only 250 miles from end to end across the water. Few distances, however, could be more deceiving, and few factoids more intriguing than this one: If all the many coves, inlets, bays, and peninsulas that make up Maine's ragged coastline were magically straightened out, the distance would instead stretch roughly thirty-five hundred miles—in other words, longer than the distance between Maine and California. And to thread your way up Route 1 along the coast, in and out of small, salty, seaside towns like Stonington, Friendship, Castine, and Port Clyde is to take in something very special—not only in New England, but in all America.

Stonington Harbor, Deer Isle, Maine Maine Office of Tourism

Located in Maine's mid-coast area on Muscongus Bay, Pemaquid Point lies at the tip of one of the coast's signature "finger peninsulas," narrow stretches of land, ocean on each side, that jut out into the Atlantic. From Damariscotta, it's a right turn off of Route 1 and another twenty miles or so down through the town of Bristol. Eventually, the scrubby pines part, and it all ends at the rocks and the little lighthouse that suddenly rises up and faces the sea. But truthfully, it's not the slight and understated lighthouse itself that accounts for the unique allure of this place. It's not bobbing boats and docks of piled lobster pots, or the tranquility of a sheltered harbor like Cundy's or Camden. Pemaquid is something more primal and dramatic. It's the way this jagged spit of land seems to know there's nowhere left to go as it winds down to the water, shaking off the last hardy scrub pines, and finally spending itself with one, last, rocky jab into the pounding surf. I've been at Pemaquid Point in different seasons; in winter, when no one's been there at all, and in summer, when visitors, cameras at the ready, straggle out onto the granite ledges to simply stand and look (often for longer than they intended) out to sea. And I always have the same feeling: *This* is the place I see in my mind when I think of the coast of Maine.

Pemaquid Point, Maine Photo Courtesy of *Chronicle*/WCVB-TV

Peter Mehegan has his own thoughts on Pemaquid. Ironically, it's here—this place of forbidding rock and crashing wave—that he's reminded of something that's often warmed him on his Maine travels.

"Pemaquid," says Mehegan, "is one of those places that give the lie to the stereotype of the unfriendly Maine native. I got to know a South Bristol lobsterman named Lewis Alley some years back, and rode with him several times while he hauled traps. Unfailingly, after docking his boat, Lewis would invite me back to his home to sample his wife's cookies and perhaps an adult beverage or two to thaw out. Lewis treated me like he'd known me all his life. But he treated everyone with the same courtesy typical of the coastal Maine native."

Pemaquid Point, Maine. Rocks, ocean, lighthouse. And Lewis Alley, and his wife's warm cookies. A-yuh.

Ultimate City Fixer-Upper: The Greenway/Boston Harbor Islands

It's rare for a place to be defined not by what's there, but by what isn't. Such is the case with Boston's newest public open space, the Rose Fitzgerald Kennedy Greenway. The contrast with what this 1.5-mile, curving slice of city looks like today and what it looked like less than a decade ago is about as dramatic a "before and after" scene as you will ever see. A truly extreme, extreme makeover. In 1959, Boston's North End, Chinatown, and the entire length of the downtown waterfront was cleaved cleanly from the rest of the city by the opening of an ugly, elevated six-lane expressway known as the Central Artery. It ran north-south through the downtown like a twisting Berlin Wall of green steel and (mostly stuck) traffic. From an efficiency standpoint, the John F. Fitzgerald Expressway ("Distressway," to a generation of frustrated commuters) was obsolete the day it opened. Decades of debate ensued about how to better move traffic through Boston's notoriously congested downtown and, as important, how to undo the unsightly scar the artery had left upon the city.

The plan? The most extensive (and expensive) reconstructive surgery ever attempted.

In 1991, work began on the infamous Big Dig, the largest highway project in US history. Over the next roughly fifteen years—and well more than $15 billion (and counting)—a 3.5-mile tunnel, at $1 billion per mile, was burrowed below the elevated highway so that it could be depressed to a wider roadway underground. ("It would be cheaper to raise the city," joked former Massachusetts

Before the Big Dig: The Central Artery, Boston
Photo courtesy of Rose F. Kennedy Greenway Conservancy

congressman Barney Frank at the time.) At *Chronicle* we did story after story on the Big Dig, sometimes focusing on mismanagement (enormous cost overruns eventually raised the attention, and ire, of Congress), but more often we focused on the grinding work itself down in the trenches, where teams of men and women worked long and hard, in often brutal conditions. The vast underground work sites were other-worldly places where the scale of what was being done was breathtaking. I remember standing two hundred feet below Boston's financial district, looking up through an enormous shaft to daylight; a subway train passed eerily overhead, while near it, a huge front-end loader was slowly lowered down from the street high above. It was surreal, like Dante doing construction.

But slowly it got done. In 2007, the Thomas P. ("Tip") O'Neill tunnel finally opened to (mostly moving) traffic. On the surface above it, section by weathered-steel section, the eyesore that was the Central Artery was dismantled. In its place, the Rose Fitzgerald Kennedy Greenway—the public's crowning payoff for the Big Dig—opened in October 2008. And it continues to evolve. Is it a perfect park? No. Nor is it finished. Criticism has seemingly been part of its blueprint from the beginning, and certainly some of it is valid. It took far too long for things to take shape. During the Big Dig, I'd always thought that fifteen years and $15 billion would be enough time and money to settle such fundamental Greenway issues as stewardship and maintenance before the project was completed. I was wrong. The Greenway Conservancy, the private, nonprofit organization responsible for growing and maintaining the park, did not even exist until 2008. In terms of design,

After the Big Dig: highway underground, new Greenway above
Photo by Alex S. Maclean

the Greenway is broken up into individual parcels, each with its own identity. It winds for just over a mile (and sixteen acres), from Chinatown, through the Financial and Wharf districts, to the city's North End. Ultimately, it's a series of "pocket parks," each with distinguishing elements, from sculpture and waving wild grass, to playful fountains and a carousel, to open-air trellises and a shallow water canal in which to wade. Trees are growing, and in the warm weather months, flowers bloom amidst cafe chairs and rolling lawns. There is, as the name quite simply demands, a real and gathering sense of greenery. In summer, there have been free concerts and a weekend open market. Food trucks have sprouted like boxy, four-wheeled shrubs along the periphery.

On a warm, sunny August afternoon in 2011, I sit on the Congress Street parcel with then Greenway Conservancy Executive Director Nancy Brennan. I recalled how high the expectations had been for this park, so dearly paid for by taxpayers. I ask her if she thought at this point, three years after opening, that the Greenway was more finished, or more "still becoming."

"Still becoming."

We watch a young couple have their picture taken near us.

"But it is also becoming part of the 'mental map' of the city for Bostonians," Brennan says. "It's a good park now—we want it to be great."

Since its opening, I've walked the length of the Greenway several times. With each visit, I feel more of a real sense of place, of an authentic park. People sit and sip coffee or eat a sandwich on benches or at small tables. (In time there'll be more shade, too.) In warm weather months, at the central Wharf District parcel, children run through the water thrown up by the playfully timed jets of water.

On this afternoon, I find myself watching, standing next to an older gentleman from suburban Swampscott, who's making his first trip to the Greenway with his wife and some visiting friends.

"What do you think?" I ask.

"I like what they did with it," he nods seriously.

Nearby, a young German couple and their daughter are resting on a low wall with their rented bicycles. The German man has the unusual perspective of someone who last visited the city while the Central Artery still stood.

"It was like a wall was here, yes?" he says in almost unaccented English. "You were afraid to cross through it, it was intimidating. But now. . . ." He spreads his arms around where they sit.

"We rode bikes along here, stop to rest at these little 'islands' along the way—it all seems connected now."

In fact, there are *actual* islands out in the harbor that are also more connected to the city now because the highway is gone. And that may be one of the greatest lasting legacies of the Big Dig and the Greenway: A city and its historic waterfront seem re-knitted together. Walk down State Street now toward the harbor and, instead of seeing a highway, you actually see the harbor. With this waterfront reconnection, Boston's harbor islands just offshore seem to beckon more visibly. This is a very good thing. Because Boston's harbor islands are a spectacular resource that had been allowed to languish in neglect and irrelevance.

"No other city in the country has this many islands so close to its downtown," observes Tom Powers, president of the Boston Harbor Island Alliance. "But for so long, the islands were a classic case of out of sight, out of mind."

Boston's Central Artery near High Street, pre–Big Dig
Photo courtesy of Rose F. Kennedy Greenway Conservancy

Actually, it was worse than that.

For the better part of two hundred years, what Boston did have in mind for its harbor islands was to treat them like dumping grounds—literally: From trash, to diseased people, to animal carcasses (a rendering plant spewed smoke on Spectacle Island), the harbor islands were places to avoid, not embrace. As a teenager, friends and I would tool around the harbor in a motorboat, stopping in at Rainsford or Lovell's Islands long enough to engage in the usual foolishness—always careful not to step in whatever yuck had either washed up or been left by the water's edge.

Today, that's all history (including the foolishness). In the 1980s, the massive cleanup of Boston Harbor began. In 1996, Congress created the Boston Harbor Islands National Recreation Area. Within the next decade, the elevated artery came down, the Greenway rolled out first a symbolic welcome mat to the water,

The Greenway today, near High Street
Photo courtesy of Rose F. Kennedy Greenway Conservancy

and then an actual brick and mortar one: The new Harbor Island Pavilion opened in the summer of 2011 as an official gateway to the islands.

From Boston's Long Wharf, regular ferry service takes visitors out to Georges Island, and then on to many of the park's other sixteen islands. On Grape, Bumpkin, Lovell's, and Peddocks, there's overnight camping in summer. And the off-shore trash heap that was Spectacle Island? More than two million tons of dirt from the Big Dig were used to permanently cap its eighty-five acres; it's now the most dramatic transformation of all the islands, with lush vegetation, a visitor center, terraced paths and walkways, a sandy beach, and a small marina for visiting boats to tie up.

In 2003, doing a story on the harbor's comeback, I spent an entire early summer day out on the water, hopping from island to island. On Bumpkin, I wandered

Spectacle Island, Boston Harbor Photo by Justin Knight Photography

past an old fort's ruins, savoring the scent of honeysuckle and beach plum, as a muffled harbor buoy clanged just offshore out in the shipping roads. Over on Spectacle, I stood on its highest point amidst waving wild grass and looked out to nothing but deep blue, open ocean. I could have been standing on Matinicus Island off the coast of Maine. Yet, turning around, there was the Boston skyline looming up over the water a scant few miles away.

"That's the thing," Tom Powers emphasizes about this remarkable closeness and accessibility. "New Yorkers can't imagine Manhattan without Central Park; fifty years from now, Bostonians will feel the same way about the harbor islands and the Greenway."

These are two extraordinary urban places made all the more so by what is no longer there—and by the fact that a city is finally getting them right.

Harbor Islands: view toward Boston, from the Brewsters Photo by Sherman Morss, Jr.

HIDDEN REFUGE IN THE CITY

The Boston Public Library is one of the city's most celebrated and admired institutions. The original was the nation's first, free municipal library. Today, at the corner of Dartmouth and Boylston Streets in the city's Back Bay, the Boston Public Library forms one handsome, sweeping, granite edge of Copley Square. Designed by Charles Follen McKim and opened in 1895, it's a place that radiates civic significance and commands respect—as do names like Plato, Galileo, and da Vinci, inscribed in stone and encircling the building's façade. But my favorite part of the library is neither visible, nor even suggested from the outside; there are no books connected with it. It's a small area within the library, and represents only a tiny slice of the building's massive, overall 930,000 square feet. But enter it once, even in passing through to another part of the building, and you will stop, and look. And take a breath. And another. The Boston Public Library's interior courtyard has that effect. It was inspired by the interior courtyard of Rome's Palazza della Cancelleria. And to lean against an Italianate pillar and listen to the central fountain gently echo off the surrounding walls, or sit with a coffee next to lush green grass, is indeed to be transported—if not to Rome, then at least far from the bustle and rush of downtown Boston. Which, incredibly, bustles and rushes only yards away, just over the wall. It's a place of instant and dramatic contrast; a place apart.

The courtyard, Boston Public Library

CHAPTER 4

THE PEOPLE

There are roughly 14.5 million people who live in New England. Through my work, I like to think I've had the pleasure of meeting a tiny fraction of them. Through good fortune, I like to think that's also included some of the most interesting New Englanders, too—with some of the best stories to tell. The following represent a further fraction of those few. In sharing their stories with us, these people left a lasting impression. Something unique distinguished them. They left us—and our viewers—immediately intrigued, sometimes moved, sometimes fascinated, and sometimes (okay, often) amused. In the sheer variety of these people and the range of their stories, they also leave a rich and lasting impression of New England itself.

Vermont Folk Hero

By the time he was seventy-five, Fred Tuttle had become Vermont's most famous dairy farmer. No small achievement in a state that, until the 1960s anyway, counted more cows than people. Or for a *retired* dairy farmer at that, with no herd and a falling-down barn. He also had poor eyesight, a mouth full of marbles, a gimpy gait, a balky heart, and a hip that needed replacing.

But then, it wasn't milking cows that made Fred Tuttle a folk hero.

We first met Fred in 1996. We stopped by his hometown of Tunbridge, Vermont, on a chilly fall afternoon, and chatted for a bit on a hilly, windswept patch of old pastureland overlooking this little Green Mountain town. We were intrigued by the buzz surrounding the recently released, Vermont-based independent film, *Man with a Plan*. We were even more curious in tracking down its unlikely star. In Fred Tuttle, we found him.

I asked him what his wife thought of the movie.

"Hasn't seen it," he said flatly, poking some leaves with his cane.

"No?" I said in disbelief.

"Nope, not once."

Fred's friend, neighbor, and the film's writer and director, John O'Brien stood by, smiling at the exchange.

"I'm sure Dottie will see it eventually, right, Fred?" he nudged softly.

"Why? She says she sees enough of me already!"

I don't know how much Fred liked dairy farming. But after five minutes of chatting that day, it was pretty clear he was enjoying this movie star thing.

"Imp-like" best describes Fred Tuttle: Short (and shorter because of his arthritic stoop), he had a rubbery-sort of friendly face, always wore a ball cap (usually emblazoned with "Fred") and large, rectangular glasses over warm eyes that seemed to be alternately opening wide, and squinting mischievously like a little

Fred Tuttle, Tunbridge, Vermont Photo by Jack Rowell

kid—which, his age aside, he seemed most like. He had a short-stepped, bowlegged walk that reminded me of Walter Brennan (himself a New Englander) in *To Have and Have Not*.

"Fred seems like he just wandered off a vaudeville stage and ended up in Tunbridge, Vermont," says O'Brien.

In reality, Fred Herman Tuttle was always very much of Tunbridge, and nowhere else. The only son of an earlier line of Vermont dairy farmers, he dropped out of school in the tenth grade, joined the army, and served overseas during World War II. He returned to Tunbridge, got married, and gradually took over his dad's dairy farm. But it was a hard life. He had two kids, then two more that belonged to his third wife, the redoubtable Dottie. His health was lousy all along. By the time he was seventy, with his own ailing ninety-four-year-old dad living with him and nursing a broken hip, and he himself suffering from severe arthritis, Fred was forced to stop farming, and

Neighbors: Fred Tuttle and John O'Brien, Tunbridge, Vermont Photo by Jack Rowell

to sell off his beloved herd of Jerseys. He needed a knee replacement; he needed money. He needed a job.

Observing all this, John O'Brien thought of the perfect job. In fantasy, anyway.

As neighbors go, Fred had others in Tunbridge whose backgrounds were certainly more similar to his than John O'Brien's. He graduated Harvard in 1985, and then returned to Tunbridge to help run his mom's small sheep farm there. But in between the feeding, herding, and shearing, O'Brien also found time to further his first love, filmmaking. O'Brien's interest is in a certain kind of moviemaking, a style he's described as "community cinema." It involves using real people, not actors, playing themselves. Essentially, it's community theater on screen rather than on stage.

"Yes, it can be rough and raw," O'Brien allows, "but when it's done well, it can have a real heart to it, in a way that Broadway often can't."

In his neighbor, O'Brien saw a rare and wonderful character to build a story around—Fred's story. So O'Brien set about writing a script that essentially mirrored Fred's life (with a central twist), and persuaded Fred to simply play himself.

"I've always said that Fred Tuttle is America's greatest method actor," O'Brien laughs. "I mean, he's been in character for seventy-five years."

In *Man with a Plan,* John O'Brien took the premise of Fred Tuttle's real-life predicament and added, well, a (fictional) plan to find the perfect job: no degree or prior experience required, a good salary, quality health care benefits, and no heavy lifting. All Fred had to do was get elected to Congress. His catchy campaign slogan? "I've spent my whole life in the barn—now I just want to spend a little time in the House."

Fred: Vermont's most famous former dairy farmer Photo by Jack Rowell

Low budget doesn't begin to describe *Man with a Plan*. Made for $100,000 (or what feature films spend in less than a month on catering), O'Brien shot it all in Vermont (with one scene in Washington, DC), casting friends and neighbors who donated their time and services. True to O'Brien's style, the film is certainly rough and raw around the edges, but full of whimsy and heart, as well as authenticity—not surprising since its "stars" are essentially all playing themselves. Fred Tuttle plods around as a most improbable candidate, and then, even more improbably, wins the election.

Man with a Plan became a cult hit, and the highest-grossing film in Vermont history. Fred Tuttle became a celebrity of sorts. He appeared on *The Tonight Show with Jay Leno* and *Conan,* sported a milk moustache on a "Got Milk?" poster, and all over Vermont, small, blue "Spread Fred" bumper stickers became as ubiquitous as ski racks.

But the Fred Tuttle story soon had a real-life second act that was even more improbable than the first. And it involved a plot twist that even the most imaginative Hollywood screenwriter would likely have dismissed as just too unbelievable.

In 1998, Vermont's Democratic US senator Patrick Leahy was up for reelection. John O'Brien had a fun, creative idea: Fred Tuttle would run for the Republican nomination to challenge Leahy. After all, there was no real threat to the popular Leahy, and the short-lived campaign would create all kinds of great publicity for *Man with a Plan.* All of which turned out to be true—wildly so.

Fred's opponent in the Republican primary, a transplanted Massachusetts businessman named Jack McMullen, was widely perceived as an opportunistic, carpet-bagging outsider who'd simply scoped out an easy race.

"So we thought, why not run a protest campaign against him?" recalls John O'Brien.

"We thought Vermont should be run by Vermonters—and what better Vermonter than Fred Tuttle?"

So, in what can only be described as an extraordinary example of art imitating life imitating art, there was Fred the candidate again, along with John, stumping around the state for real this time. Indeed, Fred's walker sported the same "Elect Fred" campaign poster that had been used for the movie; the words, "U.S. House" had been simply taped over with "U.S. Senate."

In one particularly memorable moment of the primary campaign, Tuttle and McMullen met for a debate on Vermont Public Radio. It featured the following exchange, possibly unmatched in the annals of American politics.

Fred: "This is a milk production question, Jack—how many teats does a Holstein have, and how many does a Jersey have?"

McMullen: "How many what, Fred?"

Fred: "Teats, Jack—how many teats does a cow have?"

Alas, the correct answer (four) eluded flatlander McMullen, who promptly dug his hole deeper by mispronouncing eight of the ten Vermont towns Fred put to him. Either way, the point seemed to have been made, and on September 8, Jack McMullen was defeated. Fred Tuttle was Vermont's official Republican US Senate nominee.

But the real zaniness was only just getting started.

In one of his first public statements as nominee, Fred made it abundantly clear that negative ads, robo calls , and opposition research were things that he and O'Brien would clearly not be trifling with.

"Oh, I like Leahy, he's a wonderful man," Fred happily volunteered. "I'm sure he's gonna win."

To which he added cheerfully, "But if you really want to see me go to Washington, you can always rent my movie!"

Naturally, we high-tailed it back up to Tunbridge to spend a day on the campaign trail with Fred and John. We met early on a bright, crisp morning at Fred's house. As John helped Fred into his car, I lingered on the steps and asked Dottie Tuttle for her thoughts on things.

"Well, I won't vote for him, that's for sure," she said, shaking her head.

"No?"

"No, I know that may not be fair, but he's just not qualified."

A high-pitched voice piped up through the car window just below us.

"I heard that, Dottie, I heard that!"

"He says he heard that," I gestured to the car.

"Yeah, well, he knows how I feel, and I won't leave here."

Dottie went back inside. I walked over and leaned in to the car window.

"Your wife doesn't like this political stuff, does she, Fred?"

"Not really, no; she's a wonderful person, but . . . who says I like it?"

"But you're in it."

"I know I'm in it," he said with a high-pitched giggle.

And off we went to a local elementary school where Fred would take questions from second-graders. Ken, my photographer, and I got ahead of Fred and John to get a shot of Fred's reaction on entering the classroom: In honor of their now-famous neighbor, virtually every kid in the room was wearing Fred's trademark blue jean overalls. It was quite a sight. Fred walked through the door, stopped, and stood there for a moment, astonished. He looked at John, then back at the kids, tilted his hat back on his head and rubbed his chin.

"Well, jeezum, look at that, don't you know. . . ."

The students beamed. Fred seemed to bite his lower lip. It was a wonderful moment.

The Q&A with the candidate was, well, entirely Fred-like.

"How does it feel running for Senate?" a young girl asked.

"Oh, I'm kind of a big shot now," Fred smiled.

Another student asked about the environment.

"Oh, yeah, gonna help the environment," Fred nodded.

"Another promise, Fred," John O'Brien cautioned.

"Have you made a lot of promises, Fred?" the teacher asked sympathetically.

"Too many," Fred sighed.

"How much have you spent on your campaign?" I asked Fred.

"What would you say, John—sixteen dollars?"

O'Brien nodded.

"Yeah, sixteen dollars," Fred nodded back.

The schoolchildren had their picture taken with Fred and went out to recess; I sat with him for a few moments on a pair of small desks.

"What if you're actually elected, Fred?"

"I don't know," he smiled. "My wife she'd divorce me right off quick."

"Your wife says she's not gonna vote for you."

"No, she's not gonna vote for me; I don't blame her any."

Eventually, Fred made it easy on his wife—he officially endorsed Patrick Leahy.

"I saw him at some small-town parade that fall," Leahy recalls today. "And he yelled over to me, 'Don't worry, Pat—I ain't gonna do nothin' to hurt you!'"

In truth, Leahy and Tuttle had been fond of each other from their first meeting. Tunbridge is near Ryegate, Vermont, where Leahy's mother was from. Fred knew many of the elder Leahy's friends.

Fifteen years later, speaking by phone from his Senate office in Washington, it's clear how warmly Patrick Leahy recalls both Fred and that crazy campaign. It's also clear what an uncanny and spot-on Fred Tuttle imitation he does.

"I had already committed to doing several candidates' nights with whoever the nominee turned out to be," says Leahy. "And even though Fred endorsed me, I said, 'Hey, Fred, let's go to these events together.' He said, 'Well, jeezum, Pat, oid like to, but with my hip like this, I can't droive. . . .'"

So the senator chauffeured his erstwhile opponent, and their friendship deepened. Foregoing debates, Leahy persuaded Fred to join him instead in visiting schools across Vermont that fall to speak with students. It became sort of a "Pat & Fred's Excellent Adventure."

"It was right at the height of the Monica Lewinsky scandal," Leahy recalls with relish. "And at this one elementary school, a little girl says to Fred, 'Fred, did you kiss all those girls in the movie (*Man with a Plan*)?' And Fred says, 'By jeezum, I shore did—and I enjoyed it, too!' I turned to a reporter and said, 'There's not another political candidate in America who would have said that.'"

On election night in November 1998, although he received more than 20 percent of the vote, Fred Tuttle was handily defeated by his friend, Pat Leahy.

"He called me afterward," says Leahy. "He said, 'By jeezums, Pat, I'm glad you won—I had a nightmare that I won, and I was hidin' out in the barn so no one would find me!'"

For years afterward, Leahy and Tuttle kept up their friendship. When Dottie Tuttle broke her hand, Leahy and his own wife would drive down to Tunbridge and bring supper to the Tuttles. (In Tupperware, the senator points out, so they could reheat it afterward.)

"Fred and I sat till almost midnight talking. He told me his biggest regret was quitting school; he loved children, and always told them not to do what he did, and to stay in school."

I ask Leahy what he thinks the essence of Fred's unique appeal was.

"Vermonters heard him and knew he was authentic as they come—what you saw and heard was who he was and what you got—there was no guile whatsoever, he was nice, he was warm . . ."

There's a pause on the other end of the line; the easy, self-assured voice of the nation's second-most senior senator and chairman of the powerful Judiciary Committee trails off for a moment.

"At some point before he died, he told me that the last years of his life—riding around the state, meeting school kids—were the happiest years of his life."

In 2003, at the age of eighty-four, Fred Tuttle passed away at his home in Tunbridge, Vermont.

By jeezums, he was a good one.

Forever Thirteen

The Berkshire Mountains of western Massachusetts seem more distant and removed from urban Boston than the mere two or so hours away they actually are. Single-steeple hill towns like Otis, Becket, and Monterey are splayed across the low, rolling hills. In the valleys, toughened old mill cities like North Adams and Pittsfield hang on, hugging the riverbanks of the Hoosic and the Housatonic. And in the quiet, rural middle of it, Stockbridge sits like nothing so much as a living postcard from small town America. Standing at dusk on Main Street, looking at the row of seasoned old storefronts, the long, classic porch of the fabled Red Lion Inn wrapping around the corner, and the tree-studded ridgeline of the Berkshires creating a green and gold backdrop to it all, a visitor might be put in mind of a Norman Rockwell painting. Which would be perfectly apt. Rockwell lived only a block away, and he painted that very scene.

Over the years, I've done many stories in the Berkshires. My favorite trip, though, was in the fall of 2008. We were drawn there by a couple of fortieth anniversaries. One was for a movie, the other a painting. Both involved a visit with someone memorable.

In 1969, the Arthur Penn film *Alice's Restaurant* was released. A cinematic snapshot of the 60s, the film was based on the song by Arlo Guthrie, which takes its name from the Stockbridge restaurant which, alas, is now closed and boarded up. (Guthrie, who still lives nearby in Washington, Massachusetts, and who was out of town on tour when we visited, starred in the film.) In fact, the white-frame former church in neighboring Great Barrington that figures prominently in it all is today the Guthrie Center, a local coffeehouse and performance space. In a nutshell, the song and film revolve around Arlo, a woman named Alice, the church in which Alice lives, a Thanksgiving dinner, some littering, and the cops. The cop is "Officer Obey," who in real life was Stockbridge police chief William Obanheim and was capably played in the movie by none other than William Obanheim. On a late

September morning outside the Stockbridge Police Headquarters, we reminisced a bit with Officer Rick Wilcox, who has more than a passing familiarity with the whole *Alice's Restaurant* saga. Wilcox is a strong-jawed but gentle and soft-spoken guy, with a keen view of things and a dry wit. In his office, he taps his computer, which plays the theme of the 1960s TV police sitcom, *Car 54, Where Are You.* The shelves are filled with books and photos. My eye settles on a slightly faded, framed color picture. It's a young Wilcox, in army fatigues, offering candy to a couple of Vietnamese children. While *Alice's Restaurant* was being filmed in his hometown, Wilcox was serving a tour of duty half a world away.

"Would it be safe to say," I ask, "that back in 1969, you and Arlo Guthrie were on opposite ends of things politically, socially?"

"Actually, I'd say by most political standards, my leanings are fairly liberal," Wilcox says. "But I think back in 1969, I just found the whole business a little scary, to be honest."

Chief Rick Wilcox, Stockbridge, Massachusetts
Photo Courtesy of *Chronicle*/WCVB-TV

His tour over, Wilcox eventually returned home, where something of an unlikely real-life sequel to the movie unfolded. Bill ("Officer Obey") Obanheim hired him as a rookie cop in the Stockbridge Police Department. In time, Wilcox would become chief himself. And Arlo Guthrie would become a good friend.

"This past weekend we were at the church for a concert, and he was heckling me from the stage—naturally I was heckling him back."

Wilcox tilts his hat back a bit, takes a long look down Main Street, and seems to smile at the rich irony of it all.

"Yeah, we get along just fine."

A few miles away, The Norman Rockwell Museum was also turning forty. While Rockwell did live and paint elsewhere in New England, he lived and worked in Stockbridge for a quarter of a century, and died there in 1978. In his later years, Rockwell turned his attention to the struggle surrounding racism and civil rights

Wray Gunn at the Norman Rockwell Museum, with *New Kids in the Neighborhood*
Printed by permission of the Norman Rockwell Family Agency Copyright © 1967
The Norman Rockwell Family Entities

in America. One painting from that period was of particular interest to us on that visit. It's called *New Kids in the Neighborhood* and had been commissioned by *Look* magazine for a 1967 story entitled, "The Negro in the Suburbs." In the painting, a moving van is unloading in the driveway of a suburban neighborhood. Three white neighborhood kids are warily regarding the newcomers—a young black kid and his younger sister—who look back uncertainly, with equal wariness.

"It's a powerful piece, really: Park Forest, Illinois, suburb of Chicago, being integrated, families of color moving in. . . ."

Rockwell Museum guide Wray Gunn is talking about the painting to a group of visitors who surround it, staring at it intently. They stare even more intently when their guide casually reveals that he's the young black kid in the painting.

"My grandfather Gunn said, 'You, you, and you—you're gonna pose for Mr. Rockwell, may the best person be in the painting.'"

And Wray Gunn was.

He tells us that Grandfather Gunn and Norman Rockwell had become good friends in Stockbridge.

"This man is in grandpa's house, they're talking all kinds of good stuff, they were like two kids, smoking their pipes. . . ."

Rockwell used many of his Stockbridge neighbors as models in his paintings; many more sat for initial sketches.

"If he didn't use you, he'd always be generous enough to give you the sketch," recalls Wray Gunn, now nearing sixty. "For me, I made my twenty-five dollars, and I was happy. But I really didn't understand what the meaning of that painting was. I read about it; Mom and Dad and Grandma and Grandpa told me what was going on."

But it wasn't Gunn's experience growing up in Stockbridge.

"Oh, absolutely not," he says emphatically with a wave of his hand. "We just didn't have those kinds of problems here—I went to my white friends' houses, they came to mine—but I became aware of what was going on elsewhere, very much so."

Gunn is a warm and friendly man, slight, with gray-speckled wiry hair, thick glasses, and a quick laugh. He's also been an amateur baseball umpire, and demonstrates an impressive "Strike!" call for us. When we go back inside the museum, though, and stand with him next to the painting, he's quiet for a while as he stares at it, as if alone.

"I love to hear people's interpretations of it," he says after a bit. "It's like, 'Look at the kids looking, look at the kids. . . .'"

I ask him if he's ever been to Park Forest, the Chicago suburb depicted in the painting.

"Know what? Until this last Memorial Day, I'd never been to Chicago, never mind Park Forest!" he says with a loud laugh. "I went to a Cubs game, got on the wrong subway, ended up in Park Forest—crazy, right?—I didn't stay, but I looked out the window and thought, oh, my goodness . . . so I guess I was supposed to be there at some point in my life."

"What do you see when you look at yourself in that painting today?" I wonder.

He turns back to the painting and takes a deep breath.

"Every time I see that painting I always think, 'Well, Wray, there you are—you're always going to be thirteen years old. Forever.'"

Comeback Kid

Bricklayer.

Whatever image has just come into your head, it's safe to say that Lynn Donohue isn't part of it. But then, for the last hundred years or so, her hometown's also defied easy labels.

In 1840, the New Bedford that Herman Melville arrived in (and where the inspiration for *Moby Dick* began) was already a thriving, legendary whaling port and, per capita, one of the world's most prosperous cities. In 1957, the New Bedford in which newborn Lynn Donohue arrived was already a gritty and often forlorn shadow of that earlier city. The golden era of whaling was long past, and the textile mills that followed were disappearing just as surely. The great harbor was still there, fishermen still found work, but new industries seemed unwilling or unable to take productive root. By the 1970s, a steep decline as encompassing as its earlier prosperity had settled over New Bedford. More mills and factories were shuttered, scores of store windows went dark, and unemployment, crime, and drug use rose.

Turns out, though, it's tough to sink a proud, old waterfront city—or some of its native daughters. Truth is, Lynn Donohue's own remarkable story mirrors her city's: a struggle set against tough realities, full of frustrations and setbacks, and a determination to stubbornly hang on and overcome.

We first met Lynn in the summer of 2001, as part of a story on New Bedford and its urban neighbor, Fall River. The two southeastern Massachusetts cities share similar historical arcs: an earlier "golden age" (whaling in New Bedford, textile mills in Fall River), followed by gradual decline, and present-day efforts to renew and reinvent themselves. In New Bedford that summer, there was an upbeat air in the city, nowhere more so than on the waterfront. In 1998, the city's historic district was designated a National Historic Park. It was hoped that this would help spur tourism and related revitalization, as similar recognition had for Lowell, Massachusetts. And some of that was finally happening—older buildings were being restored and redeveloped, some new shops and restaurants had opened downtown.

"We're going back to our history and bringing it forward," a developer spearheading some of the district's restoration told me. "I'd call New Bedford a real comeback kid."

You'd have to say the same thing about Lynn Donohue.

"I never thought that I was going to make it—and I made it to a degree that I have to pinch myself now."

A trim, petite woman with light, shoulder-length hair, Lynn Donohue talks fast and walks fast.

We meet up with her in the historic district, where she wants to show us some of her handiwork, and her own contribution to the restoration project. So we walked, and talked, and kept up as best we could on a street of restored, raised cobblestones.

New Bedford, Massachusetts Photo by Deborah L. Hynes

"So you actually helped lay these," I said, pausing, trying to halt her quick-step march to the sea.

"Yeah, and it was a difficult unit, too."

She stops, laughs, and holds out her hands, claw-like.

"You had to go like this at lunchtime to pry open your fingers, 'cause they would be stuck in this position."

Most lunchtimes on the job, Lynn Donohue went off to eat by herself. It was easier that way. Eventually, she would become the first-ever female member of the International Union of Bricklayers, Local 39. Her struggle, and success, would inspire others, and become the subject of a book. Early on, though, most of her future union brothers were having none of it.

I ask her if the pleasure of seeing her work is ever bittersweet, given what she went through.

"If I had known then what I know now, about how tough it would be. . . ."

Work wasn't the only tough battle. Before Lynn Donohue overcame prejudice on the job, she had to overcome a mostly dysfunctional childhood at home: four kids, little money, a bullying alcoholic father, and a working mom trying desperately to hold it all together. To escape from it, Lynn dropped out of school at fifteen, moved out, tended her dad's bar, drifted, and by her own account, was going nowhere good.

We pass an upscale restaurant; formerly it had been a seedy bar, the Pequod.

"I spent time in there, and most of my friends did, too; most of the people I hung around with were all headed on a bad path."

So was she. Lost and searching, she responded to a newspaper ad encouraging women to enter the construction trades through new regional training programs. She enrolled in a twelve-week masonry course, driving nights to a state college twenty miles away, tending bar days to (barely) pay for gas. One by one, the other women stopped showing up; Lynn stuck it out. That was the easy part. Armed with nothing more than a certificate and a resolve to "end my dead-end lifestyle and support myself," she pressed a sympathetic local union agent in New Bedford to find her apprentice work. He did. She was inexperienced and intimidated, but equally eager and determined.

"My getting into that apprentice program saved my life, and that five years in the field as an apprentice gave me the rest of my career."

But those five years in the field also tested her mercilessly. In *Brick by Brick,* a book Donohue coauthored in 2000 about her pioneering work experience, she describes in sobering detail just how jarred some men were when confronted with a young woman inching onto their turf. In hard-pressed New Bedford, union jobs were coveted, especially during the lean winter months when jobs became scarce. She was perceived by some as an interloper, a fraud. The real issue was actually a lot simpler. She was a female in a trade that was traditionally all-male.

"As I walked to my work area," Donahue wrote, "I felt the eyes of each man upon me . . . I was the 'girl,' the enemy. . . ."

Belligerent stares, ugly innuendo, and tasteless jokes were the least of it. There were also threats and jeers; there were dead pigeons left in her lunch bucket. There were also a few kindhearted coworkers and foremen who helped her along, had some human feeling for just how alone she was, and made it possible for her to keep going. But it was hard to ignore the biting and ongoing meanness. One day, she had enough; she grabbed her stuff and headed to her car. A fatherly coworker followed her and encouraged her to "suck it up" and not to quit.

She didn't. She kept her head down, showed up early to every job site, and made sure to work as hard as the hardest-working man there. Her bricklaying skills

Starting out: Lynn Donohue at work, New Bedford, Massachussetts
Photo courtesy of Spinner Publications

got better and better. She'd found a skill she was genuinely good at, and it gave her a sense of purpose and self-esteem she'd never had.

"I felt great pride in my new skills," she writes. "I was becoming the master of myself, slowly but surely."

She won a statewide masonry apprentice contest. On the job, there was grudging acceptance. There were still bumps, though. On a new construction site, Donahue was working high on a section of scaffolding that had been improperly secured; she fell twenty-three feet to the ground, gashing her head on the way down. Banged up and laced with stitches, she stayed home for a few days, and then made a wobbly but gutsy return to the work site. Even the toughest guys paused, and noticed.

"You know, it was like the real-life *Rocky* story," Lynn says now, looking back. "It really was—I just wouldn't quit on my goal; I wanted to become an accomplished, expert bricklayer so badly."

And she did.

Confident and efficient, she began taking on side jobs. Her reputation grew and so did the work. Newly married and starting a family, she was encouraged to invest in her own equipment and then, to take a leap that would have once struck her as unimaginable—form her own business. Argus Construction Corporation was notable not only because it was founded and run by a woman, not only because it did good work, but for a truly extraordinary irony: Lynn Donohue ended up hiring many of the same men who'd once belittled and snubbed her. They were now her employees. More striking still is the rare generosity of spirit with which this all played out. In being the best boss she could be—providing steady work, protecting her people, and personally delivering each weekly paycheck with a heartfelt, "Thank you"—Lynn Donohue not only made lasting friends and loyal employees out of these men, she treated them with a fundamental kindness, respect, and dignity that she herself had been denied.

Intent on paying something back to her city, she founded the Brick by Brick Foundation, helping at-risk teens in Greater New Bedford with career counseling. She began traveling frequently as an inspirational speaker, addressing schools, business groups, and women's organizations. In 1998, she went back to school, ultimately receiving her master's degree in women's studies. Today, her own kids grown, she's preparing to pursue a doctorate in education.

When we caught up on the phone, I asked Lynn if any other women bricklayers had followed her.

"In Boston, yes, but there's never been another woman in my local," she sighed. "It's tough for women now—the materials themselves have gotten so much heavier—what used to weigh seventy pounds, now weighs over ninety."

She told me about her newest effort, "The Livelihood Project," an offshoot of her foundation, in which she's using the concept of an actual builder's blueprint to help students figure out concrete steps to achieving their goals.

"I just know I want to spend the rest of my life connected with kids and education."

"And bricklaying?" I wonder. "Do you miss it at all?"

"Well, I did just do a friend's walkway."

Then that quick laugh.

"But, shhh," she adds in a playful whisper, "I told her not to tell anyone!"

My Grandfather, the President

There's just something about the town of Tamworth, New Hampshire. Maybe it has to do with its location at the northern end of the state's scenic Lakes Region. Maybe it's the way the rocky and exposed chimney-like peak of fabled Mount Chocorua soars up next to it like a three-thousand-foot signpost. Then again, it might be the series of semi-nude calendars that its townspeople have created.

We paid a visit in 2002, when "The Women of Tamworth" calendar received national attention. To raise money for various town causes, twelve Tamworth women of all ages posed tastefully but scantily clad for the camera. Heading up to New Hampshire on that trip, I piqued my photographer's attention on the two-hour drive by informing him that we'd be interviewing "Miss July."

"Sounds good," said Bob with a smile.

I neglected to add that "Miss July" was, in fact, eighty-one-year-old Ellen Eldridge.

Ellen turned out to be a hoot, and repeatedly cracked us both up.

"I think I'm old enough to do what I want to do," she grinned when I asked her why she posed for the calendar. (In her photo, she is painting. Topless.) "Besides, I thought it would be fun to do something a little hellish, you know?"

We liked Ellen.

Four years later, the calendar's creators persuaded another group of charity-minded Tamworth residents to shed their clothes: the town's men. The calendar was called, "Men in Hats," because, well, that's pretty much all the "models" wore. It was all good fun, raised a lot of money for local causes and, for a time, made the rocky summit of Chocorua only the second-most interesting exposed attraction in the area.

"You'd run into someone on the street here and, depending on what month it was, they'd say, 'Hey, I've been looking at you all day!'" laughs longtime Tamworth resident George Cleveland. "I think if you took all the calendars that were put together in this town, more people in this town have been naked more than they haven't been."

George Cleveland ought to know. He posed for the "Men in Hats" calendar, and that fall we were particularly interested in talking with him. Only in part about the calendar, though. Our interest was more about the fact that he was the only Tamworth calendar model of either sex who was a current political candidate (he was "Mr. November," naturally). George Cleveland may also be the only nude calendar model in history whose grandfather was a former US president. (In the photo, he's holding a, um, strategically positioned book.)

"Hey, none of us here has anything to hide—obviously," Cleveland says, gesturing around the village. Then he lets out a big laugh.

"Though maybe some of us should!"

Truth is, George Cleveland would have a tough time hiding anywhere. He's a big man, over six feet and not svelte. He has a round face, thinning light brown hair, and a bushy mustache. He's jovial, garrulous, has a quick wit, and is instantly likeable. We meet up with him in the center of Tamworth, which is mostly defined by a single general store. (There used to be another place next to it, a combination hardware/soda fountain known simply as, "The Other Store.") It was a chilly October New Hampshire afternoon in the eastern end of the Sandwich Mountain Range. There was still color in the trees of Tamworth, though, and plenty of life in George Cleveland's hearty handshake. It's easy to imagine that this must have been what his grandfather campaigned like, grasping hands and pressing flesh along the way from mayor of Buffalo, to governor of New York, to president of the United States. It's all the easier to imagine because, quite simply, George Cleveland is the uncanny, spitting image of every photograph you've ever seen of President Grover Cleveland. And now he, too, was running for public office. Though perhaps with a wee bit more ambivalence than his grandfather.

"The biggest thing to get used to in running is being a politician; I've never really thought of that, and now it's like, 'Eeuuw—I'm one of them. . . .'"

The 22nd, and 24th president of the United States . . . Photo courtesy of Library of Congress . . . and his grandson Photo Courtesy of *Chronicle*/WCVB-TV

Yup, right there on the ballot as a Democratic candidate for the New Hampshire State Senate. His campaign brochure is slick. George Cleveland is not slick. He's easygoing, casual and a bit shlumpy, really, and despite his political pedigree and an appealing habit of looking you right in the eye when talking, he just doesn't present overall as your average politician. ('Course, these days, that's mostly high praise.) He's wearing a fleece vest over a casual shirt and tie as we amble past the town's famous Barnstormers Theatre, the nation's oldest professional summer theater. He was the theater's longtime chairman, and was Tamworth's town moderator for twenty-eight years, his only previous political experience. He describes his professional career as "eclectic." He was program director for New Hampshire's WMWV radio station for twenty-five years. Today he's executive director of the Gibson Center for Senior Services in North Conway. He also has a regular side gig: He does a one-man show, impersonating his grandfather, and giving "tub-thumping" speeches at political dinners, schools, and historical societies.

"I put on a 'Mrs. Doubtfire' suit and gray up my hair—hey, at least I still have to do those two things!" he laughs.

George Cleveland acknowledges the uncanny physical resemblance with his grandfather—to a point.

"Yes—from the neck up."

"He was indeed a big guy," I point out.

"Yes, he was," nods George.

George Cleveland, while big, is not Grover Cleveland big. Grover Cleveland weighed over 250 pounds, and is the second-heaviest president in US history. (William Howard Taft takes the, um, honors.)

Of greater distinction is the fact that Grover Cleveland is counted as both the 22nd and the 24th US president; he's the only one to have served two nonconsecutive terms. His second and last term ended in 1897, and he died in 1908 in Princeton, New Jersey—which is part of what fascinated us about George Cleveland of Tamworth, New Hampshire: How could he possibly be Grover Cleveland's *grandson,* and not at least *great*-grandson? After all, George Cleveland was born more than three decades after his grandfather died; more than a *century* separates their respective births.

"Yes, sounds hard to believe," George concedes. "Since my grandfather was born in 1837, and I'm only fifty-four."

I ask George if he can explain the strange and seemingly laws-of-nature-defying secrets of the Cleveland family tree.

"Yes," he laughs, "I'm going to stand up now and sing, 'I'm My Own Grandpa.'" Then, without singing, he does explain.

"My grandfather was nearly fifty when he married my grandmother, who was twenty-one. Then my father essentially repeated that—he had a twenty-five-year gap with his second wife also—so we ended up dropping fifty years total. Two generations—gone!"

George proceeds to add humorous and head-scratching details, perhaps like the fact that he was born an uncle, or that his own two children are the great-grandchildren of people who are his own age. I shake my head, trying to process some of the math without a pencil and paper.

A candidate with truly nothing to hide . . . Photo Courtesy of *Chronicle*/WCVB-TV

"Yeah, it's a little weird to fathom sometimes," George smiles. "And it gets confusing at family reunions; it's a mathematical challenge."

On this day, George Cleveland needs to resume the challenge of campaigning. I ask how it's going for this descendant of one of America's most gifted and natural politicians.

"I was thinking about it for years, actually, and this time it seemed right. Look, I see something wrong and I want to fix it," he says, shrugging his broad shoulders. "I don't think I can change the world, but maybe I can help nudge things a bit."

"Has the naked calendar come up as a campaign issue?" I ask.

"If you got a problem with it, I probably don't want your vote—kidding, kidding!"

Any daydreams about following in his grandfather's footsteps to the White House? Big belly laugh.

"Not really in the cards; state senate is where we want to go."

Alas, George Cleveland lost his bid to get there. For now. But on that October afternoon, a few weeks before the election, he channels his savvy political forebear with a truly bold campaign gambit of his own.

"I challenge my opponent to a naked debate!"

He crosses his arms and smiles.

"With a tallish podium, of course. . . ."

LIFE OF A SALESMAN

Chances are, you can't easily recall the last time a door-to-door salesman (or woman) paid you a visit. Earl Goff sorely wishes it were otherwise.

"I always loved it, always a challenge," Goff smiles as if recalling the very fondest of memories.

"I loved to get out there by nine-thirty in the morning and go to the first house and then just continue, continue; people were very receptive."

They certainly were to Earl Goff, anyway. For forty-five years, he went door-to-door in southeastern Massachusetts selling Fuller Brush Company products. He was very good at it, too, consistently recognized nationally as one of the company's best salesmen. Today, he's one of the very last of his kind in New England. And although he no

Last of a breed: Earl Goff at his home "office," Rehoboth, Massachusetts
Photo Courtesy of *Chronicle*/WCVB-TV

longer goes door-to-door, Goff maintains a busy business selling the same line of products from his small Rehoboth, Massachusetts, home. Well, his tiny one-car garage, really. We stand in the doorway to it, staring in disbelief. It would seem there isn't even room enough for my photographer, Carl, to set up his camera, much less for Earl and me to join him in there.

"Yeah, it's tight," Earl agrees, surveying his compact combination warehouse, office, and mailroom. Boxes of products are stacked literally from floor to ceiling, with no apparent order or system of retrieval. L.L. Bean it isn't.

"Yesterday I had four orders," Goff beams. "I'm down at the post office everyday at a quarter to four, getting the merchandise out."

Goff has thirty thousand loyal customers, and he diligently tends to them the old-fashioned way—all of them are alphabetically listed on old-fashioned file cards. He has no computer.

"Cell phone?"

"Nope," he shakes his head. "My wife has one, though."

He laughs, and points to a calculator on the table.

"That's as high-tech as I get."

I ask him what has been the key to his success as a salesman.

"Don't be pushy," he says quickly. "You can always figure that the next time you come around, the same lady is going to order because you were so nice the first time—that was the key, having patience."

We watch as Goff patiently packs up a day's order: some brushes, a mop, a few bottles of cleaning fluid. He admits he'd rather be delivering these things himself right to the door. But at eighty-four, and with a changed way of doing business, he knows those days are over.

"I still try to get out to some longtime customers; I'll see someone in church and they'll say, 'Could you stop down?' I'll say, 'Yeah, I'll be down; might be more than a week from now, but I'll be down. . . .'"

Some things still call for patience.

Throwing an atlatl, Rindge, New Hampshire
Photo Courtesy of *Chronicle*/WCVB-TV

CHAPTER 5

THE PASTIMES

Baseball is still known as America's national pastime, though some may argue that football has replaced it in popularity. Meanwhile, the country's individual regions have their own unique pastimes as well. In Maine, for example, they race toboggans and lobster boats (not against each other). In Texas, they don't. Outdoor pastimes in New England are mostly divided neatly into "winter" or "summer" types. Which is not to say there isn't often stubborn and messy overlap in the seasons; it was a wise Vermonter who once described the state's calendar year as "eight months of winter and four months of pretty poor sledding." In our travels around New England, we've met folks into just about every pastime you can imagine. And some you likely never have. Ever thrown an atlatl? I hadn't, either. Damned near threw my shoulder out trying, though.

The Puck Stops Here. And Here. And Here.

Hockey is huge in New England, as it is in all parts of the northern United States (not to mention Canada). Indoor rinks dot the landscape from Machias to Mystic. Even better, so do outdoor ponds and lakes, which generations of New Englanders have shoveled snow off of and hovered over fires next to in order to keep warm and keep skating on frigid January nights. In the public playground behind my house growing up, the basketball court had raised asphalt edges so it could be flooded in winter for skating. After school, I'd be out there with my black and gold Boston Bruins sweater on, rushing up the ice as Bobby Orr, then deftly passing off (to myself) and brilliantly scoring as Phil Esposito. Out there alone, no goalie could stop me. And, as I recall, the cheers were deafening.

Rabbi On Defense
Photo Courtesy Elizabeth Stern

But the Bruins aside, what continually impresses me about hockey's hold on New England is how many different types of people to whom the sport appeals—people you might not expect. We met some of them in a story fittingly called, "Against Type."

It was a weekday afternoon when we first dropped by Rabbi Liza Stern's workplace, Temple Eitz Chayim in Cambridge, Massachusetts. She'd had a conflict on the morning I'd initially suggested meeting: her weekly hockey game.

"Somebody told me they heard about this team called 'Mothers on Edge'—what a great name for a hockey team, right?"

Rabbi Stern, a mother of five, had been looking for a winter sport with which she could get involved.

She'd tried figure skating, but frankly felt hockey "just looked more cool." But as she points out, it's not the first time she's gone against type.

"Actually," she says matter-of-factly, "a woman becoming a rabbi went against the popular stereotype, too."

Not that jumping in and playing competitive hockey didn't have its own adjustments and learning curve.

"As a rabbi, I'm sort of used to people treating me very nicely—they tend to watch their language, they tend to listen seriously when I say something—and suddenly I'm on the ice and I'm just someone to shove around, you know? It was a new and humbling experience."

"Any bruises?" I ask.

"You mean other than psychic bruises?" Stern laughs. "Oh, sure, sure!"

I ask her what her own family thought about her taking up ice hockey.

"I had to explain that it was a non-checking league," she says, "because when people think of hockey they think of missing teeth, so they had all sorts of ideas about how it was going to look when I was up there on the bimah, the pulpit, preaching to my congregation without, you know . . . so there was a lot of that."

At the synagogue, helping a soon-to-be young man practice for his bar-mitzvah, Stern shows the same keen focus she shows on the ice playing defense for her teammates. "I don't think they care that I'm a rabbi; I just think they think I'm Liza, and that I happen to have this other life."

More than a few members of another team we profiled can relate to that same feeling. The Lobsters, a men's recreational team, are part of the New England Senior Hockey League. Most of the team is gay.

"Everybody plays on this team for different reasons," says Lobsters left-wing Rob Meehan. "There are some people that may not have had a chance to play when they were in high school or maybe they didn't feel comfortable enough to play in youth hockey; everybody on this team has their own set of circumstances in terms of why they want to play on this team."

Why or how they ended up on this team is clearly not part of anyone's focus on the night we watch them play a (presumably) straight team at a south suburban Boston rink on a cold March night. It's a scrappy, hard-fought game for most of the first period. Taking a breather on the bench, Lobsters defenseman Sean Macamaux keeps one eye on the ice while he half-turns to talk to us.

"I've been playing hockey since I was about six years old," he says, taking a gulp of water.

Macamaux is in his late twenties, works in finance, and skates with the Lobsters two nights a week.

The Boston Lobsters pose for a postgame team picture.
Photo courtesy of Boston Lobsters

"Look," he says, "I definitely know that there's a, you know, that hockey's considered kind of a 'butch' sport; but I personally see it as two different aspects of my life that have kind of come together and they're both things that I'm fine with and it's a lot of fun."

Not that there haven't been some opposing players who've been, um, less than fine with things.

"Yeah, occasionally when we're in a more competitive game or a playoff game," Macamaux says, "and people's nerves are on edge, you may hear something a little derogatory, but . . . you'd be surprised, most guys are very, very tolerant."

Meehan, a professional who lives with his partner in Boston's Dorchester neighborhood, falls back onto the bench during a shift change.

"You know," he pants, catching his breath and unsnapping his helmet strap, "It's really a great mix of people that are really into hockey, and that's what it's all about."

He suddenly whips his head around to the action on the ice as Macamaux, sitting next to him, yells and pumps his glove in the air.

"Yes! Good pass, Bobby!"

From the ice, the air is indeed pierced by a choice expletive from the other team's goalie. But it's grunted at himself, in frustration, and it's easy to understand why. The Lobsters have scored four unanswered goals, and lead 5-1.

Have Tub, Will Travel. And Win.

When it comes to New Englanders' passions and pastimes, I've come to one overall conclusion: If something can be turned into a competition on some level, it will be. This applies, of course, to mainstream pastimes like baseball, tennis, hockey, and skiing, but also to more obscure competitive pursuits, like Segway polo, lock-picking, meat-cutting, tree-climbing, boomerangs, and belt-sander racing. All of which I've had the pleasure of watching in action. The list also includes hand tub mustering.

Chances are you've never seen a hand tub muster, or even knew that such competition existed. I didn't. But in fact, it turns out that hand tub mustering just may be the granddaddy of all American team sports competition.

"Basically, it's a competition amongst antique firefighting apparatus to see who can shoot the longest stream of water," explains David Falconi.

The "engine" in this case is nearly 150 years old, and is entirely hand-powered. Hand tubs are early forerunners of the steam engine. You've probably seen a picture or painting at some point—it is literally a huge copper tub sitting on wagon wheels, flanked by two long wooden "arms" that, when heaved up and down like a see-saw by teams of men on each side, create enough pressure inside the tub to shoot water (which can be pumped from a nearby source) through an attached hose. Ingenious. And exhausting.

We meet up with Falconi at the edge of a large field in Southborough, Massachusetts, where he and members of the Southborough Fire Department have hauled out their own prized antique hand tub, the Falcon. (I checked with Falconi—neither one is named for the other.)

There are people who are merely passionate about something, and then there are folks who are seriously passionate. Like Falconi. He's a short, fire plug (naturally) of a guy in his late fifties with a beard, glasses, and ball cap, and an energy well suited to short, decisive bursts of action, a handy trait for a former firefighter. Nowadays, he's a fire historian and all-around national expert on hand tubs. The Falcon is his baby, though, and he leads a team that competes against other tubs in musters around the country.

"We've gone tens of thousands of miles with the Falcon—we've gone out to California and down to South Carolina, just to show people what it's all about. Not everybody's seen one."

The Falcon's a thing of beauty from an earlier time, all gleaming red with handsome black and gold lettering. It was built in Boston in 1868, originally served the town of Franklin, Massachusetts, and was bought by Southborough in 1896 for $150. (A steal by today's standards; Southborough recently purchased a ladder/combination engine for $997,000.)

"There's a league rule that the engine has to be built before 1896," says Falconi. "Because at the end of the hand tub era, they were building some engines just for competition, so to speak, kind of like the NASCAR cars of today."

Falconi fusses carefully as he works to attach the hose to the Falcon. He's helped by eight members of the Southborough Fire Department who are nice enough to come along to demonstrate how a hand tub operates, and how the competition works. We couldn't have picked a better day to be around sloshing, spraying water; it's nearly ninety-eight degrees in the open sun of the bare and baking field. On the other hand, not the best day to be hand-pumping a fire hose.

"It took so many people to pump this thing," says Southborough fire captain Joe Hubley. "Doing this for an hour or more, trying to save a building, it had to be brutal."

The guys bend in and begin some practice heaves.

"What's the secret to getting this working right?" I ask Hubley.

"You have to try and get everybody working up and down at the same time; when you get the machine really rockin', you're in good synch."

Falconi, helped by his daughter, runs the hose away from the Falcon out into the field.

He eyes a spot farther out.

"That's our target," he squints and points.

"In a competition, what they do is lay out a measuring area that's eight feet wide by three hundred feet long; then they back one hundred fifty feet of hose to the engine, and you've got fifteen minutes to shoot as many times as you want."

Rockin' it old school: Southborough Fire Department and the Falcon
Photo Courtesy of *Chronicle*/WCVB-TV

"Wind must be a factor, yes?"

"Big time—when the wind's fair, you shoot it a lot; when the wind's in your face, you're lucky to get off one or two shots."

The guys are getting into it now, getting the rhythm down. It's easy to see why, from early on, pumping these things would have led to competition.

"The first official muster was July 4, 1849, in Bath, Maine—which makes New England sort of the mecca of hand tub mustering," Falconi tells us. "But the records show that there were competitions long before that—you know, if a town had a couple of engines, the natural competition was to see who was the best."

"So these led to bragging rights between cities and towns?"

"Absolutely, from the start, and it's really called 'America's oldest organized sport,' starting in 1849," Falconi says. "Before baseball," he adds emphatically.

Meanwhile, at the hand tub, the men are ready; Captain Hubley raises his hand.

"Ready . . . down—go!"

The wooden arms creak, the tub does indeed begin rocking, and the firefighters work furiously in unison, pumping up and down in what looks like perfect synch. Moments later, out at the nozzle end of the hose, there's a loud hissing, and a sputter.

"Here we go," says Falconi.

A huge, long arc of water streams up and out, hundreds of yards toward the far side of the field.

It's hard to believe it has been hand-pumped from a creaking, swaying, wooden antique. Stopping to catch their breath, some of the firefighters new to the hand tub experience can't seem to believe it, either.

"It's tough, it's tougher than you think—especially in ninety-six degree weather!" exclaims a twenty-something firefighter wiping sweat away with his T-shirt. "I can't imagine those old-timers back in the day, doing this for six hours—that's amazing. I have a whole new respect for them."

So do we. And for the Falcon. Which, it turns out, is something of a superstar in the rarified world of hand tub musters.

"It hasn't lost a muster in many years," beams Falconi, as he prepares to help his mates gently roll the Falcon back onto its special trailer. "There's just not a lot of competition out there for it."

WHEELIE MAN

I'd heard about Garth Lockhart long before we saw him in action. And when we finally did get up to Andover, Massachusetts, it didn't take long to run into locals who well understood our curiosity.

"I've been watching him for months," a Main Street merchant tells us. "First I was like, 'What the heck is going on?' I love to watch people's faces—everyone stops, everyone smiles—it's really kind of funny."

Minutes later, there he was, dreadlocks flying behind him, a huge smile and a wave to the two young boys with whom we were standing on the corner.

"What do you think about what this guy does on his bike?" I ask.

"It's pretty cool."

Yeah, it sort of is. What Garth Lockhart does is ride a bike great distances. On one wheel.

You know, the sort of thing kids do ("pop a wheelie") for a few seconds. Lockhart, thirty-three, has done it for over an hour. Which has earned him the world record.

"The kids on the street would ask, 'How long can you do a wheelie for?'" he explains by way of how this whole unusual pursuit started. "And I was like, 'Maybe a quarter mile.' And the next time they see me they say, 'How long can you do a wheelie for?' And I was like, 'Maybe a mile.'"

So Lockhart, who began hot-dogging on a bike over the hills of his native Dominica, kept pushing. And he started to eye the records. But just when he got comfortable with three miles, the record shot up from 1.3 miles in an hour, to 8.6.

"And I was like, 'Whoa. . . .'"

Consider, too, that the record was set on a controlled indoor track. Lockhart does his riding and training on urban streets, complete with potholes, cars, traffic lights—and wind.

"Once you get on one wheel, the wind can do whatever it wants with you, so it's more like a feeling game."

We followed Lockhart for most of a warm June weekday morning. Driving behind him, next to him, watching an outdoor elementary school class leap to their feet and cheer for him as he wheeled by, waving to them like a rock star.

"I love putting a smile on their face, it's better than people dying everywhere; I love to make people happy."

The Lockhart legend—and record—is now quite secure. On September 12, 2010, he set a new world record by riding on one wheel for nearly fourteen miles from Andover to Salem, New Hampshire, in just under an hour. And just for good measure, on his birthday five days later, he went out and broke his own record by doing just over fourteen miles in only fifty minutes. Not content to rest on his kickstand, he's now in training to set a new record not likely to be broken: twenty miles (on an indoor track) in fifty minutes.

My guess is he'll achieve it. He's unflappable on his bike. He's also as warm and outgoing when he's in the "wheelie zone," as he puts it, as when he's off the bike and shaking hands and giving tips to local kids. Ultimately, it's just about a simple wheelie. But Lockhart clearly sees something bigger in it all.

"It's balance," he says with his broad grin, waving his hand to encompass the busy street scene around him. "If I can balance a bicycle like that and go all the way to New Hampshire, you can balance your credit card, you can balance what you eat—it's all about balance!"

Garth Lockhart,
Andover, Massachusetts
Photo Courtesy of
Chronicle/WCVB-TV

Taking Wing

With some of the pastimes and competitive pursuits we've come across in New England, it's not that they've been entirely unfamiliar; we just didn't realize they were still going on. Like pigeon-racing. It's still going on. Not only that, it turns out there was an active club only thirty minutes from my office. Even better, in John Mathieu, we found an enthusiast with a rather expansive sense of describing this obscure pastime.

"Pigeon racing is kind of like thoroughbred horses, greyhounds, it's the same idea—it's the competition."

A short man in his sixties with a warm, crinkly face and white beard under a Red Sox baseball cap, Mathieu cradles a cooing little pigeon in the crook of his arm. He strokes her feathers gently, but his voice is animated. Misconceptions needed to be dispelled, important distinctions needed to be made, and he was the man to do it.

John Mathieu and prized racer Photo Courtesy of *Chronicle*/WCVB-TV

"These birds are not like street pigeons," he lectures, lest we confuse the club's genetically superior competitors with their dirty, distant, no-account cousins from the local landfill.

"These birds have been bred for thousands of years for speed—they can go from one hundred miles to six hundred miles in a day."

The Braintree Racing Pigeon Club is not easy to find. Headquarters is a cast-off construction trailer on the edge of the sprawling but now-mostly abandoned Quincy Naval shipyard, just south of Boston. The guys seem happy to see us, but equally surprised that we actually found them.

"Safe to say that what you guys are into could be called a fringe sport?" I ask after introductions are made all around.

"I would say it's very much on the fringe," laughs a club member. "I mean, look around you here—we're even on the fringe of the shipyard!"

Indeed, on this chilly, March dusk, surrounded by rows of darkened brick buildings with broken glass windows and sagging chain-link fences, there's a brooding sense of industrial wasteland. The only light comes from the trailer; the only sound in the air other than our voices is the soft cooing of pigeons.

Judi, my photographer, leans toward me.

"This is different."

Yes, it is.

I'm put in mind of the movie *On the Waterfront,* and the tough, tenement rooftops of Hoboken, where Marlon Brando as the young Terry Malloy kept his pigeon coops.

I ask Mathieu how he became interested in racing pigeons.

"One day when I was about thirteen, a racing pigeon had gone down. It was tired, I just happened to walk by it, and I've been hooked ever since. I brought him home, and I've been doing it for forty years and as long as I can get out there, I'll keep doing it."

Most of the men (they're all men at this club) express similar feelings and stories; they got hooked on the sport years ago and they love it. Which is good, because it's not an activity to take on casually. Nor is it cheap—racing pigeons can cost up to $5,000 depending on their pedigree.

"Three hundred sixty-five days a year, twenty-four hours a day, you gotta be there," Mathieu says. "They have to be fed, they have to be watered, they have to be cleaned, but it's what we do, it's our hobby."

"People ever think it's strange?" I wonder.

"Very," he smiles. "But in Europe it's well known."

It's a theme repeated inside the trailer. Old pictures show clubs from decades past, when European immigrants transported their zeal for pigeon racing to America. But then the Big Wane set in.

"They brought this hobby with them," a just-arriving member says, looking wistfully at a faded, sepia photo of a huge club gathering. "But it's much bigger in Europe today than it is here."

Today, the Braintree Racing Pigeon Club has fourteen members. They meet twice a week during the spring and fall racing seasons. And things have gotten high-tech. A tiny computer chip attached to the bird's foot will record its time. The night before a race, members bring their birds to the club's trailer to be weighed and tagged with a chip. The birds will stay there in cages to be picked up by a truck, which will also pick up other clubs' birds, transport them all to a release/

Winged thoroughbred Photo Courtesy of *Chronicle*/WCVB-TV

starting point that might be several states away, and then release them to begin the race back home.

"A lot of people think they fly a straight line, but they don't," points out Kevin Williams, a burly and amiable ex-Quincy cop. "They're like a sailboat, they're riding the wind."

"And covering significant distances, too?" I ask.

"Oh, yeah—I had a bird a few years ago flew four, five-hundred-mile races a season, for five consecutive years," says Williams. "That bird went to Ohio twenty-five times—I won't get there in my lifetime twenty-five times."

"It amazes me," says Mathieu, shaking his head. "This little guy went five hundred miles in one day—one day—just to come back to the love of the loft, that's why he came home."

Like golfers describing incredible shots they've seen, or fishermen reliving a memorable catch, the guys trade stories about the speeds some birds have reached.

Kevin Williams Photo Courtesy of *Chronicle*/WCVB-TV

They tell us about a recent race where birds hit two thousand yards a minute, which is seventy miles per hour. Not bad for something that weighs a pound and will sustain itself in flight for hours.

"I get in my car and drive maybe to New Jersey once or twice a year," says Williams. "And the first thought that comes to my head is, 'How are these pigeons doing this?' I have trouble driving for six hours, and they're these little one-pound things, negotiating all kinds of things, you know?"

Truth is, no one knows exactly how the pigeons do it, how they find their way back. The prevailing theory involves magnetic field and some such, but the science behind it all is clearly not of major interest to the Braintree guys. The lure is about something much simpler.

"What I love most about it is the bond that you develop," says Williams. "You raise the bird from the egg, you train it, then you sit in your backyard and watch."

Williams is pointing up in the air; in the twilight, his face brightens.

"Then, all of a sudden, this little dot shows in the sky, and your heart starts fluttering, and you think, 'Oh, I hope that's Pretty Boy.' You know?"

He smiles as he heads for the light and warmth of the trailer.

"Hey, everyone has a passion and that's my passion—some people like golf, some people like fishing, I like racing pigeons."

ROLLING ON

These days, before running through their routines, Ted Lewis and Priscilla Flynn make sure to stretch out carefully before taking to the floor. They step onto it perhaps a bit more gingerly than they used to. But then, so would you if you were ninety. Flynn? She's a mere spring chicken at seventy-six.

"My sister told me she thought it was time I grew up," Flynn says.

Lewis laughs.

"What she actually said was, 'I wish you would act your age.'"

"Yeah, 'act my age', right!" Flynn hoots.

Good luck with that.

Roller skating (not blading) is one of those pastimes you sort of know is still alive and well, you just don't know anyone who's still doing it. Now we do. We meet up with skating partners Ted Lewis and Priscilla Flynn at Roller World in Acton, Massachusetts. And we're promptly yanked back in time to the 50s and 60s—a perfect metaphor, as it turns out, for Lewis and Flynn: He didn't take up the sport till he was sixty-eight. She was fifty-four.

"It's taken a longer time because we didn't start out as children," says Flynn.

So they jumped in and kept going. After taking lessons for two years, they began competing, first with skaters of any age who'd competed for three years or less, then graduating to the "big boys," as Lewis puts it, who'd been skating all their lives. Lewis's goal was to qualify for and skate in a national competition in his ninetieth year. In August 2011, less than two months after turning ninety, he and Flynn placed twenty-first in their category (over fifty-five) at the nationals in Fort Wayne, Indiana.

"Ted is the oldest person that we know of that skated at nationals," says Lewis's coach, Bob Smith.

Ted Lewis laces up

"He still has a pretty high level of competition in him, doesn't he?" I observe.

"Listen," Smith says, "When he came off the floor at nationals, he says, 'Do you think I can beat three more people?' And I says to him, 'I'm not sure.' And he says, 'I want to be in the top twenty-five!' And I says, 'You're not making that!' But seriously, I think that's part of his secret, and I think that's what he needs to keep himself younger."

"I tell everyone that my father was ninety-three and playing golf and complaining about his score," Lewis tells us with relish. "I like that—I'm skating at ninety and complaining about not being good enough."

When the energetic pair pause for a rest, I ask the obvious.

"How do you respond to those who say, 'Hey—you're seventy-six, you're ninety—you could break something out there!'"

"You can break bones doing most anything, you can slip on the ice," says Flynn, who has in fact broken a wrist skating.

"I think if one worries about falling, you inhibit yourself, and you're more prone to fall," says Lewis, catching his breath. "So I don't even consider falling."

Flynn straightens Lewis's bow tie.

"I just want to look good," he laughs. "That's what I worry about—vanity!"

And with that, the break is over. There's a routine to polish.

Have a Seat/The Plumbing Museum, Watertown, Massachusetts
Photo courtesy of *Chronicle*/WCVB-TV

CHAPTER 6

THE COLLECTORS

New Englanders love to collect things. Anything. Not sure exactly why that is. The old stuff (antiques) I understand; after all, there's a lot of old stuff in New England. But that doesn't explain the full range and variety of quirky collections we've encountered across all six New England states. How varied, you wonder? In Erving, Massachusetts, Jeff Kaminski has planted a field full of freshly painted fire hydrants from every era going back to 1870. It's an odd sight. And there are easier things to collect; each hydrant weighs well over two hundred pounds.

"I think I may have reached my limit," Kaminski concedes.

Closer to Boston, Skip Richards's walls are literally covered with thousands of paper clips from all over the world, of every type and provenance imaginable. Cliff Wilson's Ashland, Massachusetts, barn is filled from floor to ceiling with telephone books. (Granted, a century-old directory from Paris, France, with Pablo Picasso's home phone number is pretty cool to see.) Dave ("Dr. Dave the Pinball Doc") O'Neil's basement (okay, most of his first floor, too) is lined with restored, classic pinball machines. Norman Rockwell's son, Jarvis, has a collection of tens of thousands of tiny toy figures. They fill a separate, rented space, and he often arranges and exhibits them as conceptual art installations. We've seen collections of frogs (the toy kind) that fill an attic, mini (but real) cars that fill a trailer home, and a roomful of airline barf bags (unused thankfully) from nearly every airline in the world. We've visited a tiny apartment where the furniture is obscured by a shifting avalanche of original 8-track cassettes (along with vintage players), and a home with a table-top forest of mini Jackie-O dolls, dressed in every outfit she ever wore as First Lady. And those are just some of the personal collections in people's homes.

Then there are the larger, more ambitious collections in museums. Okay, not necessarily museums with boards of directors, endowments, and glossy gift shops. Nonetheless, just off of Portland on Maine's Peaks Island, Nancy Hoffman is happy to guide you personally through the Umbrella Cover Museum ("Dedicated to the mundane in everyday life"). In Connecticut, your search for that elusive trash museum would be over. New Hampshire is home to museums dedicated to cufflinks, camping, telephones, and snowmobiles. Or perhaps you doubt that a museum could be devoted entirely to the lowly and humble shovel. So did we. But at Stonehill College in Easton, Massachusetts, I can tell you that we really dug our visit to their Shovel Museum.

At the Plumbing Museum (Watertown, Massachusetts) we found a fascinating look at the evolution of, well, just what you'd expect, as well as some unexpected

View of Stonehill College's shovel collection Photo courtesy of Stonehill College Archives and Historical Collections, Arnold B. Tofias Industrial Archives

but impassioned local pride in the region's place in it all. ("1829, Boston's Tremont House—the first hotel to have indoor toilets!") But even within this universe of unique collections, a few stand out. Which takes some doing. But then, when you lure visitors in with a life-sized Bigfoot replica, then roll out his reputed footprints and poop samplings . . . well, that's a pretty good way to separate yourself from the pack, no?

Bigfoot, Small Museum

"I put it all together," beams creator Loren Coleman. "Fifty-one years of field work, research, writing, gathering material donations—and here it is."

Yes it is. The world's first and only Museum of Cryptozoology. Right there in Portland, Maine. Sure, some people refer to it simply as the "Monster Museum." Doesn't bother Coleman.

One-of-a-kind museum, Portland, Maine Photo Courtesy of *Chronicle*/WCVB-TV

"That's okay, because 'monster' really comes out of the tradition in which people have these encounters with unknown new animals."

Which is basically what cryptozoology is all about. And which is what Loren Coleman's passion has been since he was eleven.

"I saw a movie about the Yeti, went to school the next week and asked my teachers, 'What is this about the Yeti?' They said, 'They don't exist, get back to your studies.'"

And thus, those teachers unwittingly launched an inquisitive student's forty-year obsession with things that "don't exist."

"I'm a skeptic," says Coleman who, with his salt-and-pepper hair and beard, looks like a rumpled academic at any rate. "I'm just as skeptical of true believers as I am of de-bunkers."

Either way, Coleman's humble little museum truly covers it all, from Bigfoot, Yeti, and Nessie (the big three, "Celebrity Cryptos," as Coleman calls them), to more B-List bad boys (and girls) like the Chupacabra, Fiji Mermaid, and the

Loren Coleman and his collection Photo Courtesy of *Chronicle*/WCVB-TV

Minnesota Iceman. On a huge wall map dotted with colored push-pins, Coleman eagerly points out to us confirmed sightings of specifically New England cryptids: legends like Cassie (Casco Bay sea monster), Champ (ditto, Lake Champlain), and the Dover Demon (don't ask, just Google—and note that Coleman named him. There are artifacts here from all over the world (including the aforementioned Bigfoot files), literature (including Coleman's thirty-five books), full-size cryptid models, and plenty of campy souvenir items. (Furry mini-Yetis make the cutest key chains.) The cramped and tiny museum we visited occupied the rear of a Portland bookstore; in 2009 the museum moved into a larger building in downtown Portland. Coleman continues to be founder, creative force, and your personal tour guide to this oddly compelling collection.

"It's not making a lot of money, but it's not about money," says Coleman. "It's about sharing my passion."

And with that, our tireless tour guide excuses himself to greet a young and curious couple who may or may not have simply lost their way between the bookstore's "Food" and "Travel" sections.

"Hi, folks—have you ever heard of the Campas? Campas are little, Japanese leprechaun-like creatures. If you look over here. . . ."

Unsinkable Obsession

You probably know that the legendary R.M.S. *Titanic* sank off the coast of Newfoundland after hitting an iceberg on a clear April night in 1912. You probably don't know that the home of the Titanic Historical Society and Museum is in the back of an old jewelry store in the central Massachusetts village of Indian Orchard. We enter from the front, make our way through dusty greeting card racks, past the watch repair bench, and . . . Ed Kamuda is waiting for us in the cramped, rear two rooms. Which are filled with *Titanic* memorabilia.

"They're personal treasures from the survivors," says Kamuda, a slight, soft-spoken man in his late sixties. "And we continue to amaze people when they come in here and see what we have."

"Is part of the amazement," I wonder, "that they first walk through this jewelry store?"

"It certainly is," he smiles. "It's like walking into a different world."

Inside large glass display cases are personal effects from some of the doomed ship's survivors: pocket watches, dress buttons, hair brushes, brochures and tickets, and most eerie of all, letters written and posted at the ship's last stop (Queenstown), and embossed with the red *Titanic* letterhead.

Kamuda has managed to collect these things over fifty years simply because he asked for them.

"It's amazing what people saved," he says, looking at a case, dabbing away a speck of dust.

As a teen, Kamuda saw the *Titanic* movie *A Night to Remember* at the movie theater his family owned across the street from their jewelry store. He was fascinated and began to reach out to survivors, many of whom were still alive.

"I just started writing to them," he says. "I think they were mostly amazed that someone so young was so interested in their life."

He became determined to eventually create a museum to help preserve the items people sent him. And he did. All along he immersed himself in the ship's

Remembering the *Titanic* at its one-hundred-year anniversary: Ed Kamuda, April 2012
Photo Courtesy of *Chronicle*/WCVB-TV

history, reading everything he could find, becoming a respected *Titanic* authority in the process. When Hollywood director James Cameron was preparing to make *Titanic,* he consulted with Kamuda, and also invited Ed and Karen Kamuda to be extras in a scene in the movie.

"That must have been exciting," I say, looking at a photo of Ed, in costume, on the movie's set.

"It was," Kamuda grins. "Especially having worked in the theater across the street, sweeping the floors and making the popcorn, and suddenly I'm up on the screen."

Today, Kamuda and his wife publish the Titanic Historical Society's newsletter, which reaches four thousand members worldwide. And visitors somehow find him—and his little out-of-the-way, back-of-the-store museum.

"We had one gentleman from Japan, he'd had a travel agent seek us out and he came all the way here and spent an entire day going through everything."

In addition to what's on view and open to the public in the back of the store, Kamuda also owns several larger *Titanic*-related artifacts. What he doesn't have is the

Letter postmarked *Titanic* 1912 Photo Courtesy of *Chronicle*/WCVB-TV

physical space or means to properly display them. He leaves us at one point to return to his workbench out front, where he finishes up a watch repair for a customer.

When he returns, I ask him what it is, one hundred years later, that accounts for his—and the world's—enduring fascination with the *Titanic*.

"An unsinkable ship, her maiden voyage, some of the wealthiest people in the world on board, and all of a sudden, she just scrapes an iceberg, and the whole drama begins. . . ."

And never really ends.

Wild Bill's

In Middletown, Connecticut, we found another memorable collection. Or maybe it's the *collector* who's memorable. Tough to say.

"I've never thrown anything away in sixty-two years of my life," admits Bill Ziegler. "And most of it's right here in our store."

Wild Bill Ziegler, Middletown, Connecticut Photo Courtesy of *Chronicle*/WCVB-TV

Most of it. The rest is out in back, or parked in a field, or used in decorating the world's largest jack-in-the-box, which rises slowly up and down out of an old farm silo attached to Wild Bill's Nostalgia Center. And then there's the *front* entrance, where a thirteen-foot-tall (another world's-largest) bobbing head of Ziegler himself sits on the roof. Trust me, if someone directs you down Connecticut Route 3 to this place and says, "You can't miss it," they mean it.

We couldn't miss Bill Ziegler when we saw him in person, either. (Especially since we'd already seen his giant likeness bobbing side-to-side on the roof.) He's short, wears wire-rimmed glasses, and has long, wild graying hair with a big, flowing, equally graying beard. He wears Hawaiian shirts, a permanent grin, and looks like an aging hippie, which is pretty much how he describes both himself and his customers, many of whom aren't entirely sure what to make of his store even after they've been lured inside.

"A lot of people just come in to look around and think it's a museum—that's why we had to put the sign above the door, 'Free Admission'—people were coming in and saying, 'How much does it cost to come in here?'"

Inside is a veritable shrine to the 60s and 70s (all appropriately price-tagged). A Stamford, Connecticut, blogger sums it up best in an online review:

"It's just a bizarre collection of things you might find in your grandpa's attic— If your grandpa were a biker, record collector, electronic repairman, flea-market enthusiast and pack-rat."

"It's just all the things I really like," smiles Ziegler. "60s posters, records, games, clothes—you know, the things that Boomers relate to."

Not everything's for sale. Not the original Coney Island Funhouse, which Ziegler bought some years back and now has stored in sections on his property. Definitely not his rare, original "Laughing Sal," an antique mechanized clown, which he proudly demonstrates. And probably not his car collection, which doesn't take up a lot of storage space, anyway.

"I have three Yugos; but I don't know if I'd sell one of those, either."

Carl (my photographer) and I have a ball walking up and down the aisles with Bill, checking it all out. ("Look—'Twister' in its original packaging!" Carl yells out.) We stop in the 70s clothing section.

"This is polyester heaven, Bill . . ."

"This is it," he agrees.

I try on a gray and maroon-checked jacket, with very wide lapels; very polyester, very *Saturday Night Fever.*

"It makes you want to disco, right?" laughs Bill.

I pretend to read the label: "'Don't stand too close to an open flame . . .'"

"It's you!" Bill says, arms open wide. "Five bucks and you're out the door!"

I pass on the jacket (dumb, I know), and wander around the store a bit more, getting a kick out of watching parents (and grandparents) pull things off the racks and explain them to their younger companions. ("I can't believe you never heard of the Monkees!")

Bill is off to the front counter to assist his son at the register.

"My kids work here and they never know from day to day what's gonna happen, but it will always be something odd."

I should hope so; it's not called "Wild Bill's" for nothing.

"It's you!" Rummaging through Relics at Wild Bill's, Middletown, Connecticut
Photo Courtesy of *Chronicle*/WCVB-TV

CHAPTER 7

THE CRAFTSMEN

New Englanders also love to make things. All sorts of things. From sculptors, glass-blowers, and fine furniture-makers in Vermont, New Hampshire, and the Berkshires, to classic wooden boat builders in Maine, it's a region steeped in a tradition of skilled crafts. Some of these crafts are famously associated with New England, like building covered bridges. What's less known, for example, is that there's a First Family of New England covered bridge builders.

Building Bridges: A Family Tradition

The Gratons of New Hampshire are into the fourth generation of covered bridge builders and repairers. In the fall of 2011, in the wake of Hurricane Irene, we watched Stanley Graton III working with his cousin Arnold, as they expertly patched up and re-timbered Campton, New Hampshire's historic Blair Bridge.

"It's in your blood, it's in your heritage," says Graton, as he leans out in the air, fifty feet above the Pemigewasset River, refinishing a length of original bridge truss. Now middle-aged men, both he and Arnold first worked on this bridge as teenagers, alongside their grandfather in the 1970s.

"There aren't a lot of things around that you can say you worked on that have been standing since the 1800s."

Elsewhere in New England, we've met artisans like Doug Johnson of Newburyport, Massachusetts, who makes "paintings" using only tiny colored beads. Stunningly deceptive, you're sure you're looking at a painted work of impressionism, until you bring your eye close enough to reveal the thousands of imbedded

Stanley Graton III, repairing Blair Bridge, Campton, New Hampshire
Photo Courtesy of Chronicle/WCVB-TV

beads, individually stitched onto the canvas. Karen Allen is an extraordinary knitter (and not a bad actress, either). Her cashmere creations are arranged in her small Berkshire shop as if in an art gallery. (She was happy to describe the scarf she knitted for Harrison Ford, her co-star in two Indiana Jones movies.) Then, there are the even more obscure crafts we've encountered. . . .

Blair Bridge, Pemigewasset River, Campton, New Hampshire
Photo Courtesy of *Chronicle*/WCVB-TV

A GOOD CRUTCH

Rumney, New Hampshire (pop. 1,400), is a quiet little town nestled along the Pemigewasset River Valley. A century ago, the dense timber of the surrounding White Mountains made it a prominent logging center. That same abundance of quality hardwood once made the town famous for something else, too. For a period during and after World War I, little Rumney, New Hampshire, was the world's biggest producer of wooden crutches. Today, a single roadside sign near a long-vanished mill attests to the town's former title as Crutch Capital of the World. In time, cheaper, foreign-made aluminum crutches displaced Rumney, and ultimately killed off its sole industry. In 2000, the Kelly Mill closed, ending the town's long history of mass-producing its famous product. But the mill's last owner, Ed Openshaw, wasn't ready to go quietly into the night of industrial obsolescence. So, in the crowded top-floor workshop of his home just off the town common, he makes them all by himself now.

"The mass production of wooden crutches in New Hampshire and New England is dead except for custom crutches—and I seem to be the last one making them," Openshaw says matter-of-factly, as we watch him expertly apply the finishing touches to a custom pair for one of his many customers scattered about the country.

"Customers that are on crutches for life want something nice," he says, stopping for a moment to reach down and give his dog a pat. "I've got one man in Indiana that's got eight or ten pairs I've made—wood top, leather top, rosewood, brown stain, natural—including a pair of gray stain for a gray suit he wanted a pair of crutches to match."

"Now *that's* custom."

"That is custom," he nods.

Openshaw makes about fifteen finely crafted pairs of wooden crutches a year; not enough to make a living, but enough to supplement his other work, and enough to sustain Rumney's connection to a prominent part of its past.

"How does it feel to be the last wooden crutch-maker in New England?"

"Well, I don't give a lot of thought to it, I just do it."

And with that, Rumney's last crutch-maker is back to work.

End of the line in Rumney, New Hampshire

Your Suit (of Armor) Is Ready, Sir

It was the fall of 2010. We were in New Hampshire doing a story that included a visit through the state's famed "Antique Alley." Colleen Pingree, owner of R.S. Butler's Antiques, joked, "Hey, if you want to see something really old, you should drop by my brother's place!"

Colleen's brother's place, it turned out, was not on Antique Alley. Nor does he sell antiques. But we sure thanked her later for the tip.

"People ask what I do, and I usually have to pause for a second, because it always requires a somewhat lengthy explanation."

Adam Berry has a point. I mean, how often has someone responded to your casual question, "So, what do you do for work?" with, "I make reproduction medieval armor."

Oo-kay. . . .

Adam Berry at work, Deerfield, New Hampshire Photo Courtesy of *Chronicle*/WCVB-TV

Berry's business, called White Mountain Armoury, is in his garage-turned-workshop. It's next to the small house he and his wife share high up on a quiet hill in Deerfield, New Hampshire. We pulled up, parked, and heard loud clanging. Through the open garage doors, there was Berry, hammer in hand, working on what looked like, well, what it was: a gleaming metal helmet like something out of King Arthur.

"I work mostly in mild steel," Berry explains. "Which is what cars and refrigerators are made out of; embellishments are done in brass or bronze."

Helmets are Berry's big thing, but he also makes gauntlets (as in, "throw down . . ."), which function as hand and finger protection. Don't let the "mild" steel part fool you, either.

"I have some customers who like my stuff enough to buy it and put it on their shelves, but my stuff is extra heavy duty, made to strict tolerances for groups who fight in it."

Berry does. And he literally stands behind his work, as a weekend warrior engaging in full-scale, full-dress medieval tournaments.

"So in a way, the armor is really sporting equipment—very old sporting equipment."

Only half of Berry's business is making new armor; the other half involves repairing what he's already made.

"I'm really happy when a piece comes back to me after a year to be serviced and have dents removed; it's satisfying to know it's working as intended."

"So you get stuff back," I ask, "Like helmets that have been dented where people have taken hits?"

"Oh, yeah," Berry smiles. "It's pretty amazing what can be done to them—dents, rivets get sheared off—I just repair and re-polish as needed."

Alas, not everything on the body is armored.

"Almost every time we fight, we usually have really large, purple bruises that my wife tends to find a little disturbing, but mostly it's all wear and tear on the joints similar to what a football player might have."

Now imagine football players with swords, spikes, cudgels, and lances. Ouch. Nevertheless, Berry's craftsmanship and penchant for perfection is evident. We watch him labor over a nearly finished helmet, painstakingly buffing the gleaming metal. Helmets can cost upward of five hundred dollars; a mail shirt (Berry no longer makes them) can cost over a thousand dollars.

"Armor in the middle ages was really for the society's elite; it was very expensive," Berry points out. "I have to keep it affordable for lots of college students and people who take part in this activity."

So he tries to cut down his construction time, using as many modern machines to turn his stuff out as he can. Still, we do wonder what his neighbors make of all that banging and clanging, and glinting of swords and armor out of the little garage on the hill.

"I'm not really sure anyone in the neighborhood knows what I do," Berry says, thinking about it as if for the first time. "It's quiet. I'm up here for a reason; they know there's someone up the street that taps on stuff a lot. The people at the post office must wonder what I do because I am bringing in, you know, a fifty pound box to go to Finland."

Where someone undoubtedly opens it up with relish and says excitedly in Finnish, "Honey, check out my new helmet—it's a beauty. . . ."

Vanishing Craft in Connecticut

In rural Colchester, Connecticut, there was no question we'd found the right place. There, at the end of the driveway, was the only mailbox we'd ever seen in the shape of an outhouse. (What better place for junk mail to go?) And there, on the lawn by the side of the garage, was a group of full-sized, freshly finished ones, like a small stand of very strange trees. And sure enough, another car driving by hits the brakes, and stops, and looks.

"I can't even tell you the number of people who'll just stop in," Georg Papp Sr. says. "They see one of these outhouses, and they ask questions, or they tell me stories."

Georg Papp knows outhouses. He's one of a small number of craftsmen anywhere who still make the real-deal: classic, old-fashioned wooden outhouses.

"I guess there's just a certain mystique, a certain early American charm about them."

Papp is a gentle, good-humored, bearded man in his sixties. Some years back, after becoming disabled and forced to retire from his job as a telephone installer, he decided to expand his woodworking hobby. For fun, his grown daughter asked if he'd make her an old-fashioned outhouse to add a bit of whimsy to her home in New Hampshire. So he did. Then he made another one. And even though

Georg Papp, Colchester, Connecticut Photo courtesy of Georg Papp Sr.

he intended to concentrate on building "damn good furniture," as he puts it, he couldn't ignore the effect the new outhouses seemed to have on people.

"Heads were turned. I could see that people were interested, maybe not in an outhouse, per se, but perhaps a shed that resembles an outhouse."

Now, Papp's Bull Hill Workshop (staff of one) produces handcrafted outhouses with regularity, so to speak. And they are things of real beauty, too. An irony not lost on Papp.

"In reality, in the old day, outhouses were actually pretty nasty places to go—people would hide them behind bushes, buildings, and trees—and certainly nobody wasted a lot of money and effort making one."

Now, Papp has customers like a nearby woman who made one of his outhouses the focal point of her yard.

"You know, I do take pride every time I go by that house."

It takes Georg Papp about a week or so to turn out a new piece of work. And yes, he's heard just about every joke there is or ever was that relates to outhouses.

"Although," Papp grins, "Just when you say you've heard 'em all, someone will tell me something new."

"And what about that familiar crescent shape cut into an outhouse door, Georg?" I ask. "I've heard all kinds of different things about its origins."

"Ha!" Papp laughs. "I've heard people say that it's the moon, that it represents Diana, Goddess of Women, wow. It's a handle! It's totally utilitarian. It fits your hand to open the door or hold it shut, no other reason."

Old New England Yankees, after all, were famous for their ingenuity and practicality—not flights of fancy.

CHAPTER 8

THE ENTERTAINERS

New England isn't New York, never mind Hollywood. (Which , recently, seems to have found Boston as enticing for crime drama as Capone's Chicago.) Still, a rich history of performing arts goes back a long way here. Not all the way back, mind you. The Puritans' vision of a "city on a hill" did not include a theater district. Sinful diversions like singing and dancing received rather harsh reviews—like a sit in the stocks. The Massachusetts Bay Colony was the original tough room to play. And that joyless, closed-minded intolerance didn't disappear overnight, either. Provocative (for its time) works like Eugene O'Neill's *Strange Interlude* were still being "banned in Boston" well into the twentieth century. Creativity is tough to tamp down, though. All across New England, the performing arts evolved on their own. The famed Barnstormers Theatre in Tamworth, New Hampshire, bills itself as "America's Oldest Professional Summer Theatre." In Matunuck, Rhode Island, Theatre-by-the-Sea is the nation's oldest authentic "barn" theater. (On a visit, with the ocean air wafting through the open windows, we were also treated to a barn-full of juicy anecdotes involving alumni like Marlon Brando, Tallulah Bankhead, and Groucho Marx.) In Boston during the early and mid-twentieth century, an African-American theater scene thrived, and jazz clubs like the Hi-Hat, Roseland, and Savoy Café regularly featured legends like Charlie Parker and Duke Ellington. In the Berkshires of western Massachusetts, theater, dance, and music have all grown deep and thriving roots. At its summer home in Lenox, the Boston Symphony Orchestra has made Tanglewood world-famous. Just down the road, Shakespeare & Company not only performs year-round, but its youth programs are visionary and extraordinary. The boring Bard? Hardly. I'll never forget standing in the

Lenox High School gym one evening, watching a hundred (cardboard) broadsword-wielding students excitedly choreograph a climactic battle scene based on *Macbeth*. Equally impressive is the company's work with many young first-time felons who, thanks to the cooperation of an innovative judge, have spent time in rehearsals instead of jail.

But beyond the bigger, more well-known groups, my curiosity's often been drawn to less well-known performers doing something a bit different. That describes the three that follow here. They're unique entertainers who are not easily categorized. They push the boundaries a bit, and you'd be intrigued to see them perform. The Puritans, on the other hand, would be aghast.

Escaping It All

"Michael, you just want blueberries in yours, right?"

It's an early midweek morning in Medway, Massachusetts. While Donna Purnell's kids prepare for school, she's making pancakes in her small kitchen. When breakfast is over and the kids are gone, she'll be ready to escape. Literally.

"The first thing I usually get is, 'You do *what*??'" she laughs, eyes wide. "So then I have to go into, you know, it's chains and shackles, and then they're like, 'Whoa, wait a minute. . . .'"

Which is pretty much how we felt when we first heard about Donna Purnell: Mild-mannered suburban mom moonlights as a death-defying professional escape artist. Whoa, wait a minute. . . .

"My husband—boyfriend then—had a fascination with Houdini and magic," says Purnell, by way of explaining her rather unusual career arc. "I had a pool in my yard growing up, so we would dabble with rope ties and things like that—which is absolutely not the way you're supposed to start—and we would challenge each other."

Bill Purnell, Donna's husband and coach, smiles.

"He could hold his breath longer, and he still can," she acknowledges. "But I was very good at getting out because I couldn't hold my breath as long, so I really had to get the technique down. Then we graduated from ropes to chains, then to handcuffs and shackles, and to where we are today."

Where Donna and Bill Purnell are today is building a new career. This involves spending a lot of time in swimming pools, working and re-working her underwater escape routines. It involves holding her breath for up to a minute or more, while she frees herself from a length of heavy chain in which she's wrapped and padlocked. She performs more and more frequently at public events and private functions as "Alexanderia the Great, Escape Artist Extraordinaire and the Queen of Extreme."

At home, it's just "mom."

"There's apple juice, too, Michael. Hey, girls, are you going to eat?"

What's kind of remarkable is that this is all a relatively new pursuit for Purnell. Sure, there were the Houdini escapades growing up. But that was then. Nearing forty, she was a hardworking mom of three. She and her equally hardworking husband were basically getting by. Then she lost her job.

And another job. Gone, too, was a fair amount of emotional security and self-esteem. An unsettling and unhappy period set in. She yearned to do something creative, something with passion. The idea of returning to the escape artist passion of her youth seemed crazy. It seems a lot less crazy now. It was, in fact, the escape.

"I was really looking for something else, and now I had the time," Purnell says. "My kids each have their own passions—my older daughter's a dancer, my middle daughter's a singer, my son plays hockey—and I think I've helped nurture them to say, 'You know what? It's okay to believe in something and go out and get it.'"

So mom led by example. She returned to the gym to do weight training. Steadily, she increased her stamina and endurance. She worked with free divers to build up critical lung capacity. And she met with other female escape artists to study and compare routines.

It's a small group.

"As I understand it, I'm one of four female escape artists in the world. I mean, you don't normally think of women doing this kind of thing."

As for men, I ask her about the inevitable comparisons with the most famous escape artist of all.

"Everyone idolizes Houdini, which is wonderful—he brought escapism to life. But I think after eighty or ninety years, well, I'm kind of doing something different, kind of taking his base and making it my own."

Purnell's own style emphasizes an unusual transparency. Everything is done in full view of her audience, from her preparation, to her dive in, through her underwater efforts to free herself, and surface again.

"There are no curtains, so you can see exactly what I'm doing, you can read my expressions, you can see what I'm going through."

And I have to say, it's something unusual to see. On a hot, early September day, we follow along to a local outdoor pool where the Purnells have been practicing the "Leap of Faith" routine. They first spend some time practicing breath control, as Donna hugs the pool side, head under water, while Bill kneels above her counting off the seconds on a stop watch. After a bit, as a curious crowd gathers, Bill and an assistant help Donna into a straitjacket, then wrap a series of chains around her, securing them with several small padlocks.

"I tell everyone, check the chains, check the straitjacket—I'm using Brinks locks, chains from Home Depot—it's all real, nothing's ordered special."

Her arms, I notice, are covered with angry purple welts.

"Yeah, you can see the bruises," she grimaces. "I mean, it can't be so loose it's just gonna fall off, so it really has to be restrained."

"Is there a signal if you get into trouble down there?"

Alexanderia the Great, Escape Artist Extraordinaire Photo by Meg Birnbaum

"I stick my tongue out."

"Seriously?"

"Seriously."

Is there a trick to it? I don't know. I didn't see one. And I looked. One thing's clear: In a straitjacket, with no breathing apparatus and in full view, Donna Purnell dives into thirteen feet of water chained up and weighed down. Also clear? Do not try this at home.

"If I don't get out, or my safety signals aren't read . . . there's a chance. I mean, there's always a chance.

"And doing it in the open means every time I do this it's a little different; you can't be chained up exactly the same way every time, or hit the water the same way."

"Are you afraid when you go in?" I wonder.

"There's certainly a fear factor while I'm getting all chained up and standing at the edge of the pool. But just like any athlete, if they're going to perform something, you go through your mental checklist. I literally run through all the steps in my mind—what's first, what's second—and at the same time, it's like, 'Okay, I've done this, I can do this. . . .'"

A crowd has gathered now, and stares in rapt fascination as Donna perches at the pool's deep end. Her eyes are closed; she gradually inhales deeper and deeper, closes her mouth, and then, she's in. . . .

Peering below the surface to the bottom, we can see her body writhe and twist. People's hands are over their mouths; my watch shows thirty-eight seconds have elapsed. Then forty-two. Then . . . a length of chain clearly drops away from her, then another. Seconds later, she shoots to the surface, as the crowd erupts in cheers.

She swims to the side and exchanges a high-five with Bill.

"How do you feel?" I ask her.

"I'm tired! Very winded."

She grins, as she rests her arms on the side of the pool.

"Truthfully, I still have this feeling like 'I can't believe you did what you just did.' But you know, it's such a feeling of accomplishment, too."

BTO: "Stomp" Meets Stravinsky

The BSO (Boston Symphony Orchestra) is known the world over, its season marked by sold-out performances at Symphony Hall. The BTO (Boston

Typewriter Orchestra), by contrast, does not tour internationally. It has no guest conductors, season-ticket holders, or summer home. Or regular home. It doesn't even have musical instruments. (Not as they're commonly thought of, anyway.) But like the BSO, the BTO packs 'em in, too. Even if the venues are, um, considerably more cozy.

"This is about as different as it gets," grins a gleeful twenty-something woman, tickets in hand. "And I love it!"

She and a group of friends are out on a damp and drizzly May night in Cambridge to see the Boston Typewriter Orchestra—for what she says is "about my tenth time." BTO performances are relatively infrequent, but their fans are sure to show up. On this night, it's almost an hour before the BTO's first set at Passim's, the legendary Harvard Square cafe that (as Club 47) helped serve as a launching pad for the likes of Bob Dylan and Joan Baez. But unlike any of the early folkie acts that made this tiny, basement club famous, there won't be a single guitar, banjo, piano, or harmonica in sight on this evening.

There will, however, be more Smith-Coronas, Underwoods, and Olivettis than any of those twenty-somethings have ever seen in one place before. And they will be used in ways the manufacturers never imagined. It's all been somewhat accidental, really. What's become something of a must-see act with a cult following, started out in the early 2000s purely as a lark among a couple of friends. Starting with a toy.

"I think it was sort of like a drum circle," says BTO veteran Derrik Albertelli. "With typewriters rather than drums."

But as the group experimented on their "instruments," they found they could create all kinds of percussive sounds and effects.

"We do a lot of things like propping the case open so the keys actually hit the case," says Albertelli. "We'll put copper tubing in place of the rollers—even throw bottles in there—anything that's going to provide an interesting sound."

Six or so of them together make an even more interesting sound. And become strangely fascinating, like seeing and hearing something familiar taking on a whole new life.

"When we rehearse, we analyze it, we talk about what might be interesting," says Giordana Mecagni, who has a musical background, and is the group's first female member.

"It's just this wonderful challenge to keep trying to figure out how to make this 'clack-clack-clack-ding' into something interesting and fun."

Part of the fun, too, is the stage show that goes with the noise. Wearing crisp, white shirts and thin, black ties, the group conjures an office scene out of the 50s, complete with corny and clichéd banter over the clickety-clack of the keys: Who's doing what this weekend? Anyone got that hard-to-find form for accounting, or know anything about the new girl in payroll? And who scarfed up that doughnut in the snack room?

While there's some amount of improvising, there's nonetheless a real set of percussive pieces. Most are original, although they do cover "Wipe-out" (appropriately renamed "White-out").

Many BTO members have legitimate musical backgrounds of some sort or another, and several have been in other bands. Though none get the reaction this one does.

BTO at Passim's, Cambridge, Massachusetts, May 2011

"When you tell someone you play guitar in a band, you're just another idiot with a guitar in a band," laughs Albertelli. "But when you tell them you play a typewriter, they perk right up."

Mecagni, a mom, and an archivist at Harvard Medical School, says there's often some confusion just the same.

"I'll tell people I play in the Boston Typewriter Orchestra and they think it's just a name for a band.

"'What do you play?' they ask. And I have to tell them, 'No, I actually *play* the typewriter.'"

Like concert musicians who've long grown attached to certain types and makes of instruments, BTO members swear by certain brands of typewriters.

"I'm an Underwood 5 guy now, for sure," says Chris Keane proudly.

Other members go through typewriters like guitar strings.

"I'm pretty tough on mine," admits Brendan Quigley, who designs crossword puzzles in his day job, and who seems too mild-mannered to be the typewriter-wrecker type.

Earlier, at a Monday night rehearsal at an apartment in East Boston, we'd noticed a few electric typewriters sitting in cases, unused. I asked about them. Turns out, I'd hit on a bit of an ongoing internal creative rift.

"Yeah, we have about four or five electrics we haven't broken out yet," grins Albertelli.

"Some are starting to flirt with the idea, but others are more purist, I guess."

Hey, after his early days, Dylan eventually went electric, too.

On this night at Passim's, it's a purist, "all-acoustic" set, and the audience eats it up.

"Sure, we get described a lot as a 'novelty act'," says Chris Keane. "But I like the ability to win people over every time we play."

Did You Hear the One About . . .

. . . the female Muslim stand-up comic? Who performs in head-to-toe covering? No joke. Well, actually, she's very funny.

"Growing up in Boston, we definitely felt that New England influence in our lives," Tissa Hami says onstage, holding a microphone, and nodding in agreement with a couple of young Bostonians in the front row.

"Because we weren't just Muslims, dammit—we were *New England* Muslims! We loved our lamb chowder!"

Yes, Hami is Muslim, yes, she grew up in New England, but no, this is not a woman you would expect to see onstage doing stand-up comedy. It's not what she expected, either.

"For years, friends and coworkers told me I was really funny, that I should try stand-up comedy. They'd say, 'What are you doing on Wall Street?'"

Hami laughs loudly, as we sit on the deck of her parents' home just outside Boston. It's a bright and warm late fall afternoon; in a few hours she'll be taking the stage on a comedy night at a Harvard Square club.

"I'd say, 'Are you kidding me? That's not what Ivy League graduates do. Besides, do you know how much my parents paid for my education?'"

Tissa Hami, Kansas City, 2007 Photo courtesy of Potomac Media Works

A lot, no doubt. I'm guessing that a BA from Brown University and a dual master of international affairs from Columbia and Sciences Po de Paris can't be cheap. Nor is it the usual preparation for stand-up comedy. But nothing about Tissa Hami's life has been usual. She was born in Iran in 1973. Her family came to the United States in 1978 so that her parents could pursue graduate training at Boston University. Afterward, they intended to return to Iran. But while in Boston, the Iranian Revolution broke out, the hostage crisis ensued (as did the Iran-Iraq War), and it seemed safer to stay in America. So they did, settling in the Boston suburb of Lexington. While the small town fifteen or so miles west of the city was the flashpoint for America's own revolution, that's about where the similarities ended for the Hamis and their new hometown.

"I think we might have been the first Iranians that the town had ever seen; at least it certainly felt that way."

Hami laughs, but it's clear her broader reflections are tinged with some hurt and resentment, too.

"Even now, after thirty-three years in the US, I still feel like a foreigner; something happens every single week to make me feel like a foreigner, or feel like I don't belong here. From people constantly mispronouncing my name, to constantly asking me 'where I'm really from.' It's frustrating, you know?

"Because I grew up in the US. But it's especially hard to be from a place that is generally hated and demonized by most Americans."

It was in the wake of 9/11, though, that Tissa Hami finally felt a need to do something concrete with the complex and conflicted feelings associated with being a Muslim in America.

"It was such a horrible event for all of us, and it was doubly difficult as a Muslim because not only did we feel horror as Americans, but we felt the sting of discrimination and hatred that intensified against Muslims after 9/11."

She also felt frustrated that few Muslims—and even fewer Muslim women—were speaking out.

"I thought, where are we? Why are we letting others speak for us? I felt motivated to do something, but I didn't know what. To say, 'Hey, look—we're not all terrorists, we're not all hijackers—and not all Muslim women are oppressed and voiceless.'"

In the spring of 2002, a friend of Hami sent her a magazine article about male Muslim stand-up comics.

"She attached a note that said, 'If a woman were doing this, she'd be in this article.' And I thought it was finally time to follow my friends' advice after all these years and try comedy. Once I had a vision for it—that it was a way to speak up and speak out, that it was a form of activism, that it was a way to express my ideas and thoughts—I was determined to do it. I wanted to use comedy as a tool to fight discrimination, to promote understanding between Americans and Middle Easterners, to fight the negative stereotypes, and I wanted to do it in a way that people found palatable and relatable—through humor."

"How'd your friends and family react?" I wonder.

"My friends were happy but surprised; they thought I'd never break free from the typical Ivy League path. My parents were against it. My mother is a dentist and my father has a PhD in computer science, and they wanted me to become a doctor. I had zero interest in medicine."

Slowly, her parents came around. Slowly.

"It also helped that I started to appear in newspaper stories and on TV and radio. That acceptance—and praise—from the wider community helped my parents come around."

On Tissa Hami's part, actually getting up on stage to begin with wasn't a snap, either.

"My first time onstage was at a small club in Cambridge about a year after 9/11. I was terrified.

"I had no idea how an audience would react to a Muslim woman onstage joking about things like airport security. But they loved it. I remember getting several applause breaks and I was such a novice I didn't even realize that applause breaks were really, really good and not all that common."

About five years after that, on the night we're in the audience, she does indeed get an applause break about five minutes into her first set.

"Americans have a lot of misconceptions about Islam," Hami tells her audience. "For example, in a mosque, the men pray in the front and the women pray in the back. Americans look at that and they think, 'Oh, that's so sexist, those women are so oppressed, they have to go behind the men even just to pray. . . .'"

Nervous laughter. Then the kicker.

"But we're not in the back because we're oppressed—we just like the view! We're praying for a piece of that, thank you, Allah!"

Onstage, Hami is comfortable and confident now. The audience, initially somewhat reticent and skeptical, warms quickly. That's how it usually goes for her. Even in places far from Cambridge.

"I've performed hundreds of shows in twenty-five states, many of them 'red' states, and the reaction is overwhelmingly positive—I've even gotten standing ovations in places like Kansas and Kentucky."

She concedes that she does get some negative reactions. Ironically, though, it's often from fellow Muslims.

"It comes mainly from young Muslim men who don't think I should be saying the things I say; the number of haters is small, but their voices are loud."

In 2007, Hami moved to San Francisco, "to try out a different part of the country." She's still performing, but has also moved into other areas like speaking engagements and academic workshops. She's at work as well on a book about her childhood.

"I still have those moments when I think to myself that I'm completely wasting two Ivy League degrees," she says in an e-mail when I check in with her. "And I worked really hard to get those degrees!"

There's no smiley face emoticon following that line in her e-mail. But I can hear her big, hearty laugh just the same.

YOUNG COLLEGE GUY, OLD BLUE EYES

Frank Sinatra tops few teenagers' personal playlists today—
if they even know who he is.

Sadly, according to some recent studies, neither
can many teens today identify what D-Day was, where
Normandy is, or why a beach in northern France figures so
dramatically in American history.

Jesse Garlick, however, is not like most teens.

Normandy? Knows all about it. In fact, he's been there.

Sinatra? Knows the whole songbook. In fact, he
performs it. For senior citizens. Because he likes to be able
to say, "Thank You" for D-Day, and for that generation's
sacrifice. And he likes to do it in music the "Greatest
Generation" remembers and enjoys.

Like I said, not your typical teen.

On a warm, early June afternoon, I drop in on a typical
Jesse Garlick "gig" at Cooperative Elder Services in
Lexington, Massachusetts. As I approach the open doorway
of the downstairs activity room, I hear a familiar melody
sung by an unfamiliar voice: "Come Fly With Me." Vintage
Frank, circa 1960. And the voice isn't too shabby, either.

The room is brightly lit, windows all around, and filled
with sitting men and women in their mid-to-late-seventies
and older. In Frank Berinato's case, much older. He's ninety-
five, knows all the words to all the songs, and at one point
cadges one of the nurses to help him—the easier to boogie
in the aisle. The man knows how to shake a walker.

Jesse Garlick delightedly points out Berinato to the rest
of the room.

"And his name is Frank, too!"

Berinato needs no prompting.

"That's right, Buddy!" he laughs loudly, pointing
playfully back at Garlick. "Me and Frank!"

It's not the Sands. It's better. It's a warm, wonderful,
schmaltzy scene, and I stand in the doorway taking it in
with pleasure. Garlick launches into one of my favorite

Sinatra songs, "In the Wee Small Hours of the Morning." But not before telling his audience he might get choked up a bit, because the song makes him think of his girlfriend, who's in California. Nice touch. The old ladies love it.

Before beginning "My Way," there's a sound system glitch. Garlick makes a joke about his technician.

"Sorry, folks—he's just filling in today; what can I say?"

Off to the side, the poor middle-aged guy fumbling with the wires just smiles. What's a dad to do?

"Jesse's a special kid," John Garlick tells me afterward. "And I like to think I say that not just as a proud father; I really do admire him so much."

Growing up in Brookline, Massachusetts, Jesse Garlick spent a lot of time with his grandmother, Anita. She'd

Sinatra lovers: Jesse Garlick and friends
Photo courtesy of Cydney Scott/Boston University Photography

worked for the war effort, and her stories about that period and her passion for Frank Sinatra all rubbed off on her young grandson. He loved the crooning music she played for him, and was fascinated by the stories of her generation's sacrifice and simple, everyday heroism. When he was seventeen, he persuaded his dad to take him on a trip to Normandy to better understand the events he'd only read about or seen in pictures.

During a break at the Senior Center, Frank Berinato tells Jesse Garlick about his own World War II experience. He was at the Battle of the Bulge, and barely escaped an incoming German shell that killed several of his buddies. But the two also laugh about loving Sinatra.

"What's your favorite song, Frank?" asks Jesse.

"'Under My Skin!'" says Berinato brightly. "Love that song!"

"You got it," says Jesse, as they shake hands warmly.

"I get that every time I play for people like Frank," Garlick says quietly, shaking his head.

"It's why I do it."

Jesse Garlick has no illusions about a career in singing. He's got a pleasing voice, doesn't try to mimic Sinatra, but has clearly absorbed the essence of "Ol' Blue Eyes." When he graduates from Boston University, Garlick plans to pursue an acting career. And keep performing for seniors whenever he can.

"If I ever win an Oscar," Garlick laughs, "I will sing, 'My Way' instead of doing a boring 'Thank You' speech."

As I'm leaving, Berinato grabs my arm.

"Hey, come to my big birthday party this summer!"

He tells me a local bank has offered him a hundred dollars if he reaches a hundred.

"Hold out for a grand, Frank!"

We laugh.

"Love this song," says Berinato, turning to the front of the room where Jesse Garlick has begun singing, "Young At Heart."

"And I love this kid!"

The iconic dome of the Massachusetts Institute of Technology, Cambridge, Massachusetts
Photo Courtesy of *Chronicle*/WCVB-TV

CHAPTER 9

THE NERDS

Wicked "Smaht"

By 2008, when *Chronicle* did a story on the subject, "geek chic" had already become a relatively mainstream phenomenon. Once the very definition of unhip, to be a "nerd" was suddenly a very hip thing indeed. Not to mention a cool theme on which to base movies, TV shows, and national magazine articles. Who were we to ignore it?

(A note about terminology: Among those we spoke with who self-identify, the terms "nerd" and "geek" are often used interchangeably.)

To be sure, nerds and geeks are everywhere. Always have been. (What else was Galileo, the "Father of Modern Science?") Apple was born in a garage in suburban Los Altos, California. Bill Gates may have spent some time in Cambridge before dropping out of Harvard, but he'll be forever associated with Seattle. Facebook founder Mark Zuckerberg is from New York, although he also spent some time at Harvard. (Just ask two of his classmates, Cameron and Tyler Winklevoss. . . .)

All that said (and Silicon Valley aside), Boston is in many ways the nation's nerd capital. Thinking—brain power—has traditionally been as much a natural resource in New England as corn in Iowa or coal in Pennsylvania. Indeed, universities and research institutions are as ubiquitous in the Boston area as oil derricks in Texas. It's been that way for centuries. For sure, Philadelphia and New York were significant cities during America's early struggle for independence. But Boston was indisputably the emerging nation's intellectual hub, and John Adams its leading thinker. (Granted, that Jefferson guy from Virginia was no dummy, either.) While he later moved to Philadelphia, Ben Franklin was born in Boston in 1706. Let's face it, with his thick glasses and passion for science and inventing things, Franklin was not only a Founding Father but clearly the nation's Founding

Nerd as well. Had such gadgets existed, Franklin would have been undoubtedly scurrying around Independence Hall, assisting others in uploading their photos, updating their Facebook status ("Newly Independent!"), and live-tweeting from the Constitutional Convention.

"With all the leading academic and research institutions, high-tech companies, you name it, Boston is an epicenter of geeks," says Gracie Sanchez.

Better known professionally as "8g," Sanchez and her brother Rik have made Boston home to Sanchez Circuit; they describe it as a "science and technology-inspired clothing and design company." (From its mission statement: "Our dream is to outfit . . . the known nerd universe. . . .") At their small Watertown studio, there are plenty of pocket-protectors in every conceivable color and style. But my eye falls on a black T-shirt which looks like a wearable blackboard, and is covered with tiny, famous formulas. Turns out Newton and Einstein can still attract controversy.

"They've been calling it a 'crib sheet,'" says 8g, "because it has everything on it from Maxwell's Equation to photosynthesis."

"Would that not be allowed to be worn during an exam, for example?"

"Well, there was one kid online," she says, "He said he was made to take his shirt off before class."

"Cheating?"

"I don't think he was cheating," she smiles. "If he's a true geek, he wouldn't need to cheat."

Geek Pride

Other examples abound of Boston being Nerd Central. And MIT—geekdom's Taj Mahal—is only part of it. For example, Boston College has gained a national reputation as a sports power. But it isn't football or basketball that fires up professor John Gallaugher.

It's a very different type of BC Eagle pride he preaches.

"I am a geek—and that is a badge of honor!" he loudly and animatedly proclaims in front of an early-morning class. "I love technology and it's okay to admit that now because the pocket-protector crowd has finally gotten some respect!"

Gallaugher turns down the lecture-room lights; a projection appears and covers the hanging screen in front of the class.

"Look at the Forbes 400 list of the wealthiest people in the United States; it's loaded with technology folks—Bill Gates, Paul Allen, Larry Ellison, Michael Dell—geek, geek, geek, right down the list. You should feel empowered by the geekdom that you see up here! It should give you the geek goosebumps!"

Back in his office, Gallaugher, an earnest and amiable middle-aged guy with a gleaming skull, bright eyes, and a ready smile, spreads his hands in the air as if to encompass the world.

"The argument can actually be made that we're all geeks now, especially the younger generation," he says excitedly. "We organize our lives around several technologies—e-mail, texting, etc.—and that is inherently geeky if you have to press several keys to get a letter to show up in an arcane language on a tiny screen; it's all geeky stuff and everyone does it."

Gallaugher also writes a popular blog, "The Week in Geek," which serves as a bridge of sorts.

"A lot of geeks don't understand business, and a lot of business people don't understand technology; that's what it's all about."

John Gallaugher teaching at Boston College: "I am a geek—and that is a badge of honor!"
Photo Courtesy of *Chronicle*/WCVB-TV

MIT: MASSACHUSETTS INSTITUTE OF TUMMLERS

In Yiddish, a "tummler" (TOOM-ler) is loosely defined as one who is "lively, prankish, or mischievous." To the nerdy bastion that is MIT, one can only say, "Mazel-tov" (congratulations) for achieving a higher level of tummling than any other major university anywhere. (I'm told the education's not bad, either.) Truly, though, MIT does in fact have a rich history of great minds, great research—and some really, really great pranks.

It begins even before reaching the campus itself. As you approach the school and the Cambridge side of the Massachusetts Avenue Bridge (which spans the Charles River, connecting Cambridge with Boston), there is an official-looking, yellow Pedestrian Crossing sign. Students doctored it to read, NERD CROSSING.

But nothing compares with the school's long and celebrated tradition of "hacks": the large-scale, ingenious, and intricately designed pranks that are pulled off with the planning and precision of a covert military operation. Going back over a century, hacks at MIT have inspired books, a website, even a permanent exhibit at the MIT Museum ("Hall of Hacks") just to more properly commemorate some of the more legendary ones. That would include the large, black weather balloon that MIT pranksters succeeded in having pop up through the field itself during a Harvard-Yale football game in 1982. It stopped the game, as it rose up from the ground and slowly inflated. Then, as players and officials stood by in mute bewilderment, it exploded in a cloud of harmless white powder. Good stuff. (Plus, MIT loves sticking it to their more stuffy academic neighbor down the street.)

The huge, iconic dome on MIT's central building (see photo on page 142) has long been a favorite target for hacks. On a sunny, spring morning in 1994, the school woke to find a full-size replica of a campus police cruiser sitting on top of the dome like a mammoth hood ornament. (It was complete with a uniformed, dummy "driver" which, from the ground far below, looked eerily like the real thing.)

"That might be my favorite hack ever," says Samuel J. Keyser.

Keyser, a big, cheerful teddy bear of a man, has a rather encyclopedic knowledge of MIT hacks.

Which seems only right. In addition to being a professor of linguistics and philosophy, he also holds what might be the only university chair anywhere specifically endowed to encourage humor on campus.

"Hacks are for MIT what football is for the Big Ten," he laughs. "Plus, I really think there's a tacit contract between the faculty and students that hacking is okay."

If such a contract does exist, students certainly don't refrain from testing its provisions.

In 1990, on his very first official day as MIT's incoming president, Charles V. Vest was being ceremoniously escorted to his new office. Trouble was, his escorts couldn't find it. That's because it had been hacked—the entire section of hallway wall where the office's entrance stood had been completely covered over and camouflaged to look like one, long bulletin board.

"The funny thing is, there's no organization," marvels Keyser. "Where do they come together?"

"Where do *you* think they come together?" I ask.

He leans in conspiratorially.

"Well, MIT is a honeycomb of tunnels underground, and I think they meet in the tunnels. . . ."

We ask Keyser for a few of his favorite all-time hacks.

"I'm big on dome hacks; certainly the police cruiser was a great hack."

Another favorite dome hack involved a full-size telephone booth being placed on the top of the dome. On its discovery, a campus police officer was sent up on a long extension ladder to the roof in order to take a closer look. He was in for an additional surprise.

"Just as he reaches it," Keyser says excitedly, "the phone rings! He gets on his walkie-talkie, radios the chief, and says, 'Chief—the phone's ringing! What do I do?' And the chief says, 'Well, answer it!'"

Keyser laughs uproariously.

To be sure, MIT has helped birth some pretty big things, like the Ethernet, artificial skin, voice recognition technology, and the fax machine. Not bad. But ingenious and unforgettable hacks? Now, *those* are some heady achievements.

Nerd Hip-Hop

For other geeks, it's all about the music. Their own music.

"The pat answer is, it's music for geeks by geeks," is the way Ken Leavitt-Lawrence, of Gloucester, Massachusetts sums it up.

"I think it was inevitable with the advent of more powerful computers which allowed production to be done in the home which can rival these big studios. You got a lot of nerds in front of their computers—it was only a matter of time before some of them were going to start singing about stuff that was interesting to them."

Which is what Leavitt-Lawrence did, joining other nerds in shaping a sub-genre of hip-hop called "Nerdcore." (Leavitt-Lawrence is also featured in the 2008 film, *Nerdcore for Life,* which bills itself as "a documentary about nerds, geeks, dorks and the hip-hop they make.")

Musician and Muse Photo Courtesy of *Chronicle*/WCVB-TV

Sitting in Leavitt-Lawrence's cluttered Gloucester apartment he shares with his wife, it's hard to know where to let my gaze fall first. Computers and recording equipment fill his small "studio" nook. But so do pictures and memorabilia related to his music muse—renowned British physicist and cosmologist Stephen Hawking.

Leavitt-Lawrence records as his alter-ego, MC Hawking. On the wildly popular CDs and animated videos he's produced, Leavitt-Lawrence turns Stephen Hawking into a rapping superhero, saving the world through brains as much as brawn.

"I decided early on that the songs were all going to be about science and how awesome he is," says Leavitt-Lawrence almost apologetically. "I wouldn't be making fun of him—he'll always be the guy on top, you know?"

But early on, some feedback arrived from overseas. And not the good kind.

"A newspaper contacted me who talked to somebody at Cambridge University where Stephen Hawking teaches, and said that while he hadn't talked to Hawking about it, he couldn't imagine Stephen Hawking would be happy. And I thought, 'Oh, crap. . . .'"

But the day after Leavitt-Lawrence took the call from the newspaper, he received another communication, which seemed to reinforce Stephen Hawking's reputation as not simply a genius, but a genius with a real sense of humor, too.

"It was an e-mail from Stephen Hawking's personal assistant," smiles Leavitt-Lawrence, as relieved in the retelling as he must have been in the initial reading of it.

"It said that he'd seen it, and thought it was just hilarious."

"So Stephen Hawking himself saw your video?"

"Yes, and a few people later told me that he's brought it up himself during lectures."

"How does that feel?"

"To me," Leavitt-Lawrence says, shaking his head in amazement, "just the fact that there's any amount of this guy's—potentially the smartest person in the world—any amount of his brain that's dedicated to thinking about this stupid little website and music I've got going on . . . it's just hilarious."

Searching for a Deeper Online "Connection"

But while nerds have found themselves making their own music, fashion, and becoming unexpectedly cool in general—they seem to have some difficulty sometimes finding, well, *each other.*

Like thirty-something Scott Josephson. Slight, soft-spoken, and personable, Josephson's a self-described "geek" who, he confides, lives a very fulfilling life, save for love.

"Romance is sort of the one thing I am missing from my life," he shared with us on a visit to his condo north of Boston.

He gets claustrophobic in bars, he tells me. But he cautions us not to pigeon-hole nerds and geeks as being guided by intellect only.

"I think geeks are driven by passion, not always reason or logic."

If Josephson *does* venture into a bar, he could employ a rather unique opening line.

"I'm watching all the episodes of *Star Trek* in the order that they aired on television."

Hey, sure beats, "What's your sign?"

Equally frustrated in finding love among the nerds was the young woman in her late twenties we spoke with who found—surprise, surprise—that men were frequently intimidated by her intelligence.

So were we.

"I'd meet a guy at a party," she explained, standing in the lab where she was working.

"And inevitably it comes up, 'Oh, what are you studying in graduate school?' 'I'm studying intra-molecular vibrational energy redistribution of small poly-atomic molecules using ultra fast lasers.'"

"And what would they say?" I wondered.

"'I think I see my friend—nice meeting you!'"

Enter to the rescue, for nerds everywhere, Joyce Dales.

"Geeks may be shy and introverted," Dales tells us, "But they do not enjoy anonymity—they want to be known by other people who appreciate what they do and what they're all about."

Dales, a Maine native in her late thirties, was one of the lucky ones in love. She and her husband met through a conventional online dating site in 2003. Today, they're raising a family in Nottingham, New Hampshire.

"It wasn't so easy to find a fellow geek; it took many frogs before I found my nerd prince."

But she lamented her brother James's lack of success with dating. Our visit with Joyce Dales is actually at her brother's unusual antique and curio shop in Eliot, Maine. ("The Bizarre Bazaar—where the Eclectic Collect.") James models an authentic Darth Vader helmet for us.

"He had even been rejected by e-Harmony," his sister tells me. "For not being conformist enough in his profile."

I get an inkling of what she means.

"I think we all just want to live in a galaxy far, far away," James says through the thick, black mask.

Perhaps. But all alone?

So, motivated partly by her brother's dating plight, Dales and her husband decided to do something about it.

Joyce Dales, "Sweet on Geeks" website founder Photo Courtesy of *Chronicle*/WCVB-TV

"We were talking about none of the current large dating sites fit our needs as geeks, and we joked, 'Well, we've got the skills, we should start the site, ha, ha, ha.' And we did."

They launched "Sweet on Geeks" in 2007.

"It's an online place for geeks, nerds, dorks, and dweebs to meet other people who love and appreciate them," says Dales. "You can be completely honest about what you're passionate about as a geek—you can say, 'I'm into *Star Trek*' or, 'I like *Dungeons and Dragons*'—you can be sincere about these types of things and you don't have to look at more superficial aspects."

The site took off, and now counts more than thirty thousand members from across the United States and around the world. (Where else will you find ads from Mensa?)

"About three years into the project, we began to hear reports of engagements, and then weddings," says Dales. "We even have someone who will officiate geek weddings!"

"What's the long-term plan, fantasy, expectation?" I ask.

"Complete world domination. We're heading that way, anyway—the geeks are taking over, you know."

Perhaps love really does conquer all.

CHAPTER 10

THE FOODS
Wicked Good

While it's true that I've traveled and worked my way around New England, it's also true that I've pretty much eaten my way around New England as well. (There's nothing worse than reporting on an empty stomach.) Sure, a lot of stops are simply about sustenance, but many others have been "working lunches" (or breakfasts, or dinners), where the eats have been part of the story. So while I wouldn't describe myself as a foodie, I do sort of play one sometimes on TV.

On the road, my culinary radar is generally fixed to a certain frequency. I'm rarely in search of haute cuisine; simply hot cuisine is often enough. Besides, the people, places, and stories I've usually pursued have mostly been quirky and offbeat. Why should the food be any different?

I would add, however, that when it comes to food, too quirky and too offbeat can be too much. The perfect example of which is a Providence College professor we met—a gracious and earnest young man—whose guiding passion is persuading people that eating insects is the way to go and the wave of the future. I can report that, after sitting in his kitchen and sampling sautéed locusts with a side of ants, it is neither the way to go, nor something you want in your future. (And no, it didn't taste like chicken.)

Today, New England is certainly more of a contemporary food mecca than it was even thirty years ago. That's great. Bon appétit. But it's the homemade, homegrown dishes that New England's always done best that continue to capture my fancy. I know a great clam chowder when I taste it. And I'm delighted to say I know where the best cup in New England can be found. Hot dogs may not have been invented in New England, but the bun you think of eating one in was. America's *best* hot dog? You'll find it next to a tiny parking lot on the edge of downtown

Boston. Go figure. And the most iconic and colorful symbol of American road food—the diner—was, in fact, born in New England, and has often been a staple of my stories from the road.

The fact is, food tells its own flavorful story about New England. From crab cakes to pancakes, I not only think of the food itself, but often I remember the place I ate it, the people who made it, the people who served it, and others who sat around me enjoying it. It's not surprising to me that I do; it's one of the best parts of my job. What surprises me is that I don't weigh four hundred pounds.

The Choicest Oyster

Always go with local eats. You visit Memphis, you want ribs. You visit Maine, you want lobster. And so you shall find it. You'll find it steamed in the shell (or

Perry Raso on his farm, Matunuck, Rhode Island Photo Courtesy of *Chronicle*/WCVB-TV

out); in pies; in bisques and stews; on rolls and on pasta; and inside casseroles, fritters, and raviolis. Lobsters are caught off the New England coast from Maine to Rhode Island. But so are other shellfish, from clams and quahogs, to scallops, mussels, and oysters. Not to mention a vast variety of fish. Needless to say, there's a correspondingly vast variety of places to eat all this seafood.

Boston's full of 'em; so's Cape Cod. Some are quite good. (Many aren't.) On Boston's Fish Pier in the Seaport District, working boats still tie up and fish is still processed, but little else (like the daily fish auction) remains of the pier's bustling heyday. One living relic, though, is the No Name, which started as a diner there in 1917, and endures today as two floors' worth of a busy, noisy seafood circus, still drawing as many locals as tourists at lunchtime.

In Matunuck, Rhode Island, we were lured by oysters.

We tagged along with Perry Raso as he made his way out to his Matunuck Oyster Farm, and so can you. Raso is a big proponent of aquaculture, and takes folks out on a shallow, protected estuary where he's been farming oysters for ten years.

"It's like rows and rows of corn at a corn farm," he explains, as we hang over the side of his boat, peering just below the surface at the rows of sturdy, plastic mesh bags that contain the growing oysters.

"They can double or triple in size within just weeks."

The farm is now harvesting up to half a million oysters a year. Which is welcome news onshore at Raso's accompanying restaurant and raw bar.

"It's like farm-to-table, but on the water," he smiles, dumping out a fresh batch of oysters.

A "Chowda" to Savor

Now, make no mistake, oysters are delicious. But just as many a Memphian has long sought out their definitively favorite rib joint, I have long quested for that "best" cup of clam chowder. (I'll never turn away from a promising lobster bisque, either.) I found it on the outskirts of Brunswick, Maine, at a tiny little place called the Gurnet Trading Company. It sits on a stretch of Route 24 above a small inlet called Buttermilk Cove. The place was formerly a junkyard—literally—until Julie Soper and her husband, Brian, who's also a commercial scalloper, bought it and fixed up the place.

"People thought we were crazy when we bought this," Soper says. "But we had a vision."

So they spruced up the small triangle of land above the water and by the side of the road, and set themselves to making good seafood as only someone with their pedigree could. Julie Soper, a short, middle-aged mom with long, light hair and a warm but no-nonsense manner, is the seventh generation of a Maine fishing family.

"My dad was a ground fisherman, and so were my grandfather, and my great-grandfather, and all the way down through the line, and I'm the first fish-dealer," she laughs. "But I get seasick, so this helps—I like my feet on the ground!"

Back in the tiny kitchen, behind the equally tiny counter and the three-table "dining room," Soper's feet are firmly on the ground, but they don't stay in one place long; she darts about the space while her hands work frantically. That vision

THE chowder, Gurnet Trading Company, Brunswick, Maine
Photo Courtesy of *Chronicle*/WCVB-TV

she and her husband had now entails a fresh fish and lobster market, offering eat-in or take-out staples like clams, scallops, and the biggest (and tastiest) haddock sandwich I've ever seen. On some days, Brian Soper will drop in with fresh scallops just off his boat.

"People will eat 'em raw right out of the bucket," Julie says. "I'm not a big scallop eater, but they're good!"

And then, there's the clam chowder: meaty, delicious broth that's thick but not floury, with lots of whole clams, and without a lot of useless potatoes gumming up the works. My search was over. Carl (my photographer) and I put our stuff down and took our time devouring a couple of cups. Slowly. Which suits Julie Soper just fine.

"I pretty much tell people if they're looking for fast food, they better go up the road three miles because they're not getting fast food here!"

No, you're not. So relax. And savor.

Speed Dog

While finding that best cup of clam chowder had become something of a quest for me, others have set their sights on other tasty targets. Like journalist and author Raymond Sokolov. Unlike me, Sokolov seriously knows his way around food. He's a former restaurant critic and food editor for the *New York Times,* and has written several cookbooks, including *The Saucier's Apprentice: A Modern Guide to French Sauces.* But for all his high-falutin' haute-cuisinin', Sokolov has also nourished (and fed) a much less fancy food obsession since his childhood in Detroit: He loves hot dogs. In 2008, Sokolov wrote about his nationwide search for the best hot dog in America. It took him from Los Angeles to Chicago, and on to the East Coast. I would have happily wagered Sokolov in advance that he'd taste no better dog anywhere than the Boston Speed Dog. And as it turns out, he didn't.

Sokolov anointed Speed's "The dog against which I now measure all others." He also describes Speed's as "an expression of New England: dour setting, cerebral ambience, no frills." All of which is true.

I first sampled the Speed Dog in 2000. A friend and colleague of mine had been insisting I had to check out this small hot dog truck in Boston's Newmarket Square, a gritty industrial expanse surrounded by the city's meat and produce district. Speed, I was told, had irregular hours, no phone number, and there was no way of knowing if he was there or not on any given day except by calling one of the businesses on the Square, asking them to look out the window, and visually confirm whether or not Speed's truck was there. I finally went down there, and I understood. Then I returned with a photographer so I could share the experience with our viewers. I stood alongside the small chrome counter, on the other side of the tiny cramped quarters of a small trailer, and watched the long-running chore-ography in action. Speed, in his eighties at the time, moved with calm, quiet, but deliberate precision. Tall, wafer thin, with shiny, mocha-colored skin, big round glasses and an ever-present blue baseball cap, Speed gently turned the eight-inch, all-beef dogs on the grill, along with the fresh buns. Some say his nickname had

Speed Dog alfresco

to do with being a former fast-talking DJ. Maybe. Speed never said. What he was always happy to share, however, was the process by which he made the extraordinary hot dog over which you were salivating.

"You got to marinate it in apple cider and brown sugar, then charcoal-grilled over real hickory wood chips to give it that picnic taste, and of course served on a special Speed Dog roll—then add your Speed Dog mustard, BBQ sauce, relish, onions, and chili—all special made for the hot dog, and it all goes back to the days when I was working on dining cars for the railroad."

When a dog was done, Speed would spear it with a long knife, expertly slicing it down the middle, and add his unique sauces and fixings before handing it across

Ezra Anderson, aka "Speed" Photo Courtesy of *Chronicle*/WCVB-TV

the open window to another patiently waiting customer, who would then devour it with near-reverential (you'll pardon the pun) relish.

"It's better than a steak!" gushed a middle-aged businessman with a loosened tie on a sunny, June lunchtime at the Speed wagon.

But you needn't take his word for it. There's the ex-con's testimonial as well.

"I've been coming here for twenty years," the businessman smiled. "One day, I was here chatting with Speed, and this guy comes up and Speed says, 'Hey, I haven't seen you for quite a while, where you been?' And the guy says, 'I just got out of Walpole [state prison] this morning, been there for five years, this is my first stop—I've been thinking about these dogs every minute!'"

That's customer loyalty.

In 2008, Ezra Anderson turned things over to his longtime associate, Greg Gale. Fans miss the slow-moving, gentle and stately presence of Speed himself. But the essential hot dog he created is still served up in the same place, and devoured with the same gusto. What Speed said years ago when I asked him how he regards his customers' happy, messy faces, still holds true.

"That's my reward," he smiled laconically, seemingly unfazed by the long line beginning to snake around his trailer. "When you see someone who's never had one enjoying it, and you hear 'em eating 'em . . . ."

He paused, looked out past the crowd at his counter, and then turned back to business on the grill.

"Well, you may go through New England eating hot dogs, but you won't find one of these."

No. You won't.

Sweet Breakfast in Sugar Hill

Sugar Hill, New Hampshire, is one of those places that, quite simply, sums up a certain sense of what New England is all about. Sitting on the edge of the White Mountain National Forest, hard by a couple of fabled notches, Sugar Hill is surrounded by several mountain ranges, and is dotted with old, white wood-frame houses and fading red barns, all colored in by the rolling reds, greens, and yellows of tall, spreading hardwoods and evergreens. Sugar Hill itself was officially incorporated only in 1962. But New Hampshire's newest town nonetheless has a history that is old and rich. Nestled next to Lovers' Lane, you'll find the site of

America's first ski school. Along a winding dirt road with a wide open view of the Kinsman Range and Mount Lafayette, you'll pass an old, battered mailbox with the name "Frost" still visible on it. Just above it, in the small and simple white farmhouse, Robert Frost lived for five years, raising a family and writing poetry. (On warm days, Frost would prop his bare feet up on a front window sill; neighbors walking by would notice them sticking out and remark, "He's working.")

Just down the road from the Frost place is Hildex Maple Sugar Farm, continuously occupied by the same family since 1819. At the top of a hillside, facing a rolling meadow and the mountains across the road, is a rustic red and white timber-framed building. Constructed in 1830, it was used in the past as a carriage shed and to store firewood. In an effort to help sell their maple products during the Great Depression years of the 1930s, owners Polly and Wilfred ("Sugar Bill")

Breakfast time at Polly's, Sugar Hill, New Hampshire
Photo Courtesy of *Chronicle*/WCVB-TV

A CUP OF COMPROMISE, TO GO

In Montpelier, Vermont (the nation's smallest state capital), you won't get lost looking for a Starbucks. On the other hand, you won't find one, either. But just yards down State from the diminutive state house, you will find a Montpelier mainstay, a unique and independent coffee shop with the most patently perfect name: The Capitol Grounds Café.

"You get to know the legislators, the news people—it's a spot you're gonna run into everyone at one time or another," says owner Bob Watson.

You will certainly run into Watson. A sixtyish boomer with a bushy mustache, wire-rims, a Red Sox cap, and a perpetual smile, Watson seems more like the blissed-out crunchy types who moved to Montpelier in the 60s than any common caricature of the flinty, taciturn native Vermonter. But he grew up in Montpelier, and his family goes back six generations here.

"It's a real community," Watson says surveying the scene along the street. "It's genuine, it's real, and the people who are here really like it here."

They certainly seem to like the natural gathering place that the Capitol Grounds has come to represent. Regulars range from local office workers, to college kids and other young people, to legislators who use the place as the office there's no room for at the tiny state house down the street. All of which makes the people-watching here as good as the coffee. Which Watson is a bit of a fanatic about. His nearby roastery keeps the shop stocked with over twenty-five different coffees from around the world. In a wonderful bit of whimsy, the cup sizes complement the ever-present whiff of politics here. Forget "small," "medium," or "large"; never mind "Tall," "Grande," or "Venti." Instead, the cups cross the political spectrum: "Conservative," "Moderate," "Liberal," or "Radical."

"Most popular size, Bob?" I wonder.

"'Liberal,' by far," Watson grins. "But we do have a lot of conservatives come in; they do want a larger coffee, but they shy away from saying, 'Liberal.'"

"It's not easy, after all."

"But we give them an out," Watson says brightly. "We say, you can call it, 'Large' or 'Sixteen Ounce,' and everyone's happy."

Message from Montpelier: We can overcome partisan gridlock. One cup at a time.

Where a "conservative" is on the left Photo courtesy of Bob Watson

Dexter converted the building into a small tearoom and began offering waffles, pancakes, and french toast to lure customers. "All you can eat for 50 cents," they advertised. It worked. Three renovations and three generations later, the flapjacks have never stopped flipping at Polly's Pancake Parlor.

"Mother made the pancakes on little sandwich toasters," laughs Nancy Aldrich, whose parents flipped the first flapjack here. "She'd bring them out in sets of threes, which is what we do today."

Make that *lots* of sets of three—nearly two thousand pancakes are served at Polly's on a busy day.

"We had one gentleman who did eat sixty pancakes," says Nancy's daughter Kathy Cote, who's now running Polly's with her husband.

"Sixty? In one sitting?" I ask, in disbelief.

"One sitting. But his trick was he didn't use butter or syrup."

Why eat pancakes then?

For one thing, the maple syrup at Polly's (not surprisingly for a maple sugar farm) is outstanding—clear and fancy-grade only. (They make a delicious maple spread as well, but most pancake purists miss that.) The pancakes themselves are light and perfectly golden, offered in several varieties of grains, all stone-ground at the farm. They'll add in fresh blueberries, walnuts, or shredded coconut.

The dining room itself, lined with huge windows, looks out at the mountains. I've noticed on my visits, though, that people tend to look down at their plates more than out at the view.

"It's like going to your grandmother's house, it really is," an older woman visiting from Maine tells us as we sit outside on a clear, chilly October morning. "Because you get the pancakes, and they bring them hot, and then they bring the next batch—just like home."

A couple from Georgia asks if I'd take their picture in front of Polly's.

"We heard about this place for years," the gentleman gushes. "We heard about it, read about it, saw it on TV—this is like a pilgrimage!"

Eventually, we follow them in and are reminded all over again just how, well, heavenly the pancakes are. In their book *Roadfood* (something of a bible for me), authors Jane and Michael Stern describe Polly's as "maple paradise." And truly, on this crisp fall morning, settling inside with the warmth and sweet aroma, the trees outside ablaze with foliage as low-lying clouds lift off the mountains, it's hard to imagine a lovelier place in the entire world to eat a pancake.

Or sixty.

Diners: A New England Specialty

If you know your diner lingo, you'll easily translate "Adam and Eve on a raft" as "two poached eggs on toast." (Want them scrambled, instead? Add, "Wreck 'em." See? Now you, too, can speak "Dinerese.") What's not to love about a good diner? Gourmet or health food it usually isn't. Filling and delicious comfort food it often is. And these days, sometimes more. Davis Square's **Rosebud Diner** in Somerville, Massachusetts, is that rarer exception—an authentic, streamlined diner (fully restored and listed in the Register of National Historic Places) that also offers an eclectic and somewhat non-diner-like menu. (You'll search a bit before finding another 1940s-era diner that serves fine wine and microbrewed beer.)

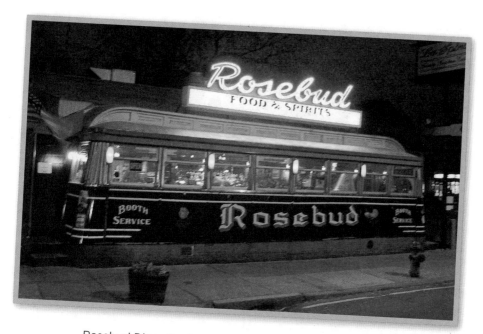

Rosebud Diner, Davis Square, Somerville, Massachusetts
Photo by Elizabeth Thomsen

It's just that quality that owner Becky Rand tells me she loves most about her own place, **Becky's Diner,** which sits right on the waterfront in Portland, Maine, and attracts a busy and diverse crowd, from fishermen in the pre-dawn, to local professionals and tourists throughout the busy day.

"You might have a CEO sitting next to a bag lady," Rand smiles, looking at the large, horseshoe-shaped counter. "Everyone's welcome."

The classic diners—all neon, stainless steel, swiveling stools, and big, plate-glass windows—often jump out like rare gems in an otherwise ordinary street scene. Good diners are about good homemade food and a living link to an authentic slice of Americana. (No less so than the apple pie you'll find at any diner worthy of the name.) A morning coffee at the counter preceded by a friendly, "Menu, hon?" Not a bad way to start the day. In the evening, on the road, you don't have to be a nighthawk to feel the lure of a lit-up diner beckon invitingly like a living Edward Hopper painting.

Boulevard Diner, Worcester, Massachusetts Photo by Andrew F. Wood

To be sure, diners aren't nearly as common as they once were. If there was an endangered species list for eateries, diners would be the functional equivalent of the Snail Darter. Fortunately, however, the retro trend over the past twenty years or so has saved some old diners and spawned some new ones. New England is particularly lucky, in that several great, old diners survive in all of the region's six states. Partly, that's because the diner was essentially born here. In the early 1870s, a young newspaper pressman in Providence, Rhode Island, named Walter Scott began selling food to night-shift workers from a horse-drawn wagon. The innovation caught on. In time, the horse was dispensed with, and the wagons got roomier and more specialized. Eventually, many "wagons" dropped the wheels, too, and became fixed locations. As demand and popularity increased, companies like the Worcester Lunch Car Co. began mass-producing the ever-sleeker and more customer-friendly diners (which took the actual name from the railroad cars they'd begun to resemble). It's been a long time since new diners rolled off the line in Worcester, Massachusetts, but the state's second-largest city still boasts several surviving historic ones, like the **Boulevard** and the **Miss Worcester.** (The "Miss Woo" actually sits across the street from the original site of the Worcester Lunch Car Co.)

Breakfast in a Classic, Worcester, Massachusetts
Photo by Vera Kaufman

"Miss Woo": the genuine article, Worcester, Massachusetts Photo by Vera Kaufman

In nearby Watertown, Massachusetts, the **Deluxe Town Diner,** which began serving hardworking locals in 1947 (as simply the "Town Diner") has preserved much of the original architecture (tiles, neon, stainless steel), while broadening its menu (falafel, cappuccino, vegan burger) so far beyond standard diner fare, that an original "Town" customer reading it now might wonder if it was printed in a foreign language. On the other hand, the meat loaf dinner, pot roast, and homemade crab cakes would all be comfortingly familiar.

But while the quality of the food counts, for sure, the essential appeal of a diner for me has more to do with what it represents than what it serves. There's something wonderfully democratic about diners. Everyone's thrown in all together. Diner counters are great equalizers—you might end up squeezed in between a trucker and a teacher, or a student and a stockbroker. That just doesn't happen as much at the Savoy or Le Cinq. (Well, the stockbroker, maybe.)

Main Street Station Diner

Elsewhere today, a genuine Worcester Lunch Car remains an emblem of truly authentic diner history.

Genuine Worcesters are often sought out by buyers, and owned with pride. Just ask Steve Luce.

"Worcester diners have always been intriguing to me," says Luce, inside his very own. "It has a real niche in this town, it's a really comfortable place to come to, and it's a real gathering place for locals."

Luce owns the Main Street Station Diner in Plymouth, New Hampshire. Known in earlier decades as Fracher's, it was built in 1946, brought up to Plymouth in 1948, and bought by Luce in 2007.

While doing some stories in the Plymouth, New Hampshire, area, my photographer, Carl, and I drop in to the diner on a chilly and rainy October morning. Along with a steaming mug of coffee, the dark wood paneling, cozy booths, and original wall sconces add glow and warmth.

Main Street Station Diner's original 1946 interior, Plymouth, New Hampshire
Photo Courtesy of *Chronicle*/WCVB-TV

It's a mixed breakfast crowd for sure—a mom and toddler, two professional guys having a meeting, a few other locals reading the paper over their eggs, and several college students in sweats who've wandered over from the campus of Plymouth State University across the street. Surveying the scene from a quiet corner booth, I ask Steve Luce what his own thoughts are on the enduring appeal of a diner.

"I think it's the uniqueness," he says after a sip of coffee. "I think that's what makes a diner a diner—it kind of stands by itself, and people enjoy that. Look, in a hustle and bustle world, you come in here, and you kind of say, 'Wow . . . this is a little bit different . . . you know?'"

I do know. I also know now that I can't finish a whole plate of pancakes at Steve's diner, mainly because they are the size of my head. (Well, that and also the fact that I'd already sampled a hefty ham and cheese omelet.) Carl, however, does finish his entire order, and promptly announces, as is his custom, "No lunch for me."

He has lunch.

Two at the counter at the Main Street Station Diner, Plymouth, New Hampshire
Photo Courtesy of *Chronicle*/WCVB-TV

Agawam Diner

This gleaming chrome diner sits at the intersection of Routes 1 and 133 in Rowley, Massachusetts. I first began dropping by in the early 80s, on trips to nearby Plum Island in Newburyport, and Crane Beach in Ipswich. The Agawam's history is so long and so complicated that it would take a genealogist to accurately explain it. On the back of the diner's menu is a "History" page. By the time you get to "Agawam #4," you're excused if you're confused. Let's just say that today's Agawam Diner has a family of direct diner relatives, some still in service elsewhere on the North Shore. It was built in 1954 by the Fodero Company of

Agawam Diner, Rowley, Massachusetts

Bloomfield, New Jersey, and was moved to its present location in 1970. It's still owned and run by the Galanis family, which traces their first Agawam diner to 1940 in Ipswich. Inside, it's simple and classic-looking: a long counter with padded stools, and a row of roomy, wood booths all by the large, front windows. The booths all have small, original jukeboxes; they hadn't been working for a number of years, but were fixed recently. Otherwise, locals and longtime customers would be hard-pressed to find much new or different. But that's the whole idea.

"Diner people tend not to like change," smiles Angela Mitchell, daughter of owner Andy Galanis. "And we haven't changed much!"

I hadn't been to the diner for a while, but on a recent visit, menu mainstays like meat loaf, corned beef hash, chicken pot pie, Yankee pot roast, and the hot turkey sandwich stare back from the page at me like warm, familiar faces. Which is something Angela Mitchell, who started working here as a cashier in high school, knows something about.

"I love working out front," she says. "I love the people, the long-time customers—same guys come in at breakfast, same guys at dinnertime—they have the same stool, same booth. . . ."

We're chatting at the counter, where a discussion has commenced between customers about what makes a good high school coach.

"What do *you* think?" Angela says, as other heads turn in my direction.

"Hm, I think I'll need some coffee for that one."

It's only mid-afternoon. The meat loaf will wait; I settle for a coffee and a slice of banana cream pie. All is right with the universe.

Red Arrow Diner

Not every diner looks like, well, a diner. True, for most folks, the image that comes quickest to mind is that diner classic of the 40s and 50s—all sleek, silvery, and streamlined, with a polished counter, tile floors, and bright naugahyde booths. With perhaps a smart-alecky short-order cook named Ernie, and a gum-chewing waitress named Flo with a pencil through her bun. (Or was that in a movie I saw?) In reality, plenty of eateries take the name "diner," while their physical look, shape, and style take many different forms. The Red Arrow Diner in Manchester, New Hampshire, is one of those. Physically, it's a short, squat brick affair, and will never win any beauty contests. But never was the phrase,

"It's what's on the inside that counts" more true. The Red Arrow is a beloved institution in Manchester going back to the early 1920s. In fact, New Hampshire's "Queen City" once sported a full quiver of Red Arrows; at one time there were fully five of them scattered about this former mill town on the Merrimack River. But by 1987, the lone, surviving diner on Lowell Street had closed, and the book on the long Red Arrow story was in danger of closing for good as well.

Enter a plucky and enterprising sparkplug named Carol Sheehan, whose family already ran a nearby restaurant. Along with her dad and another partner, she bought the vacant diner, refurbished it, and began a steady process of injecting it

Survivor: Last of the Queen City's Red Arrows Photo by Vera Kaufman

with new life and energy. For a small place, it hops. It's fun. The menu has all the diner standards; the baked beans and meat loaf are both made from the original eighty-year-old recipe that Sheehan found during the cleanup. But there are also unique touches—especially at breakfast—like the pork pie and eggs (Carol's grandmother's recipe), or the crab cake Benny. And while the official Hostess Twinkie may have lived its last (does a Twinkie really die?), the Red Arrow does its own version—"Dinah Fingers"—and makes more than five hundred of them a week.

The food and the fun, however, are only a part of the Red Arrow's reputation. Perhaps owing to its local popularity, it's also become an obligatory stop and photo op for political candidates out foraging for votes every four years in the run-up to New Hampshire's first-in-the-nation presidential primary. Sheehan's seen pretty much every candidate you can think of come through her diner at one point or another over the past thirty years or so. She doesn't say where her own political leanings lie, but she's pretty clear about which candidates impressed her as diner-goers.

"Hillary Clinton . . . she actually looked you in the eye when she shook my hand—which most of them do not."

"What'd she eat?" I wonder.

"I think it was a tuna melt."

Not keeping score here, mind you, but it was another Democrat's visit (former New Mexico governor Bill Richardson) that reminds Sheehan of something funny.

"He *loved* our bacon," Sheehan recalls with obvious amusement. And understatement.

"He had two orders of just bacon!"

Richardson didn't win the New Hampshire Democratic Primary. I'd like to think, however, that he at least got the pork producers' vote.

Last Call

"Man does not live by bread alone; frequently there must be a beverage."

—WOODY ALLEN

It's no surprise that Boston is home to a lively mix of popular and even storied Irish pubs. But there is only one Doyle's. Except for a dry spell during Prohibition, the "juice" (as former owner Gerry Burke, seventy-one, calls it) has flowed

Local landmark: Doyle's in Jamaica Plain Photo courtesy of Doyle's Cafe

here continuously since 1882. And in truth, the "dry spell" was hardly dry; Doyle's was a speakeasy during Prohibition. Over 130 years, the landmark tavern at the corner of Williams and Washington Street in the city's Jamaica Plain neighborhood (J.P. to locals) has been owned by only two families: the Doyles and the Burkes. (Gerry Burke Jr., forty-one, took over with a business partner in 2005.) Step through the old, wooden door on Williams, and you're surrounded by an eerie mix of a present that's familiar (Sam Adams beer, Wi-Fi, flat screen TVs), and a past you've seen mostly in black and white photographs, rows and rows of which stare back at you from the walls: Curley, Collins, Kennedys, and other legends of Boston politics, all having tarried here. (Some tended to tarry longer than others.) The old tin ceilings, long, original bar, dark wood booths,

History on tap at Doyle's . . .

red-and-white-checkered tablecloths, and the ghostly, pervasive presence of patrons past all make this the very picture of what central casting sees when it thinks of an authentic Boston pub. (Literally—Doyle's has appeared in more movies and commercials than many working actors.) In short, history's on tap as much as the beer here. And it flows as freely. Especially from the elder, amiable, and semi-retired Burke, a short and spry man with a shock of white hair and a face that quickly lights up with laughter. Burke, who now calls the place his "club," is blessed with an abundance of that quintessential Irish "gift of gab." Each story seems to recall another, even funnier one. Ask him about his favorite James Michael Curley anecdote. (The punch line involves a free paint job for the roguish former mayor.) Or even better, the colorful story behind the bullet hole high on a wall (now cleverly camouflaged by the circle of the moon in a Paul Revere mural). Yet all this fabled past doesn't turn Doyle's into some musty museum with a menu and a liquor license. It is still very much a happening and inviting gathering place for a notably diverse mix of people.

"We're the consummate neighborhood bar," says Gerry Sr. "But not strictly an Irish bar—we're the greatest melting pot in the city."

That hasn't always been the case in some of the city's other traditionally tight and insular neighborhoods. And it didn't happen at Doyle's by accident.

"My grandfather, my father, and my brother Eddie and I operated the refreshment concessions at Franklin Park," Burke told a gathering in 2005, when asked about Doyle's well-deserved reputation for being welcoming and inclusive.

"We worked with everybody up there. And we never forgot how oppressed the Irish had been in their own day, and that always guided us in dealing with people."

Even so, broader changes in Boston's neighborhoods—particularly in J.P.—have helped as well. Decades back, Doyle's, like most every other working-class, hard-boiled bar scattered across the city, was grittier, tougher, and all male.

"Years ago," recounts Gerry Sr., "We'd announce 'last call,' and guys would say, 'I'm not leaving—what are you gonna' do about it?'"

"Nowadays," laughs Gerry Jr., "your grandmother, or somebody else's, might be sitting in the next booth—and you better be okay with that."

Father and son smile and shake their heads over what the regulars of yesteryear might make of the place today. After all, the official name now is "Doyle's Pub & Cafe," and the menu includes more chi-chi than shot n' beer items, like the broiled citrus Atlantic salmon and veggie quesadilla.

"In those days, you just needed a plain, old cook," laughs Gerry Sr. "Now you need an executive chef."

"Hey, don't forget the sous chef!" his son adds with a grin.

In fact, Doyle's even attracts (gulp) tourists today.

"God love 'em," Gerry Sr. says. "You walk in my door, you're conferring an economic benefit on me."

Still, his son concedes that some of his older regulars worry about the tug of change in this living landmark.

"Sure, they'll say to me, 'Hey—you're not gonna go all *Cheers* on me, are you?'"

An older, distinguished gentleman making his way out after lunch waves over to the Burkes.

"Nice to see ya, Tommy!" dad says, waving back. "How've you been?"

The gentleman makes a detour for our booth, and he and the elder Burke chat warmly for several minutes.

"Look, you live and die with your regulars," continues Gerry Jr. "You can't ever forget where you came from."

The Burkes come from J.P. From the neighborhood. And even with all the changes here, their place at Williams and Washington seems to stay true to itself.

"Lot's of people hate going to work," Gerry Sr. says, spreading his arms and gesturing around us.

"I always loved it."

The lunch buzz over, the Doyle's large, front room lapses into mid-afternoon quiet; early spring sunlight glances in through the windows. Gerry Jr. is up to do some work; there's a business to run. Dad crosses the room, and with a hearty Irish laugh and a warm handshake, greets another familiar face. There's a peal of laughter, and a hand on the shoulder.

I sense a story coming on.

POSTSCRIPT: A BIG BOOK (NO, NOT THIS ONE)

When it comes to stories I've covered, one of my all-time favorites involves a book. Or, to be more precise, the effort to create one. Not just any book. What caught my interest in 2006 was a project aimed at making the biggest book in the world. Pretty ambitious stuff. Especially for fifth graders.

Indeed, the Big Book project seemed so fascinatingly audacious that I couldn't resist checking back in on it repeatedly over the years. So I did.

It all grew out of English teacher Betsy Sawyer's after-school writing club at the Groton-Dunstable Regional Middle School in Groton, Massachusetts. It didn't start out big, though.

"The idea originally" recalls Sawyer with irony, "was to help kids write and create some *little* books."

Instead, her students hatched the idea of creating something much, much larger. A world's record, they learned, would mean making a book at least twelve feet high and ten feet wide. Not wanting to dampen their youthful enthusiasm, Sawyer changed the club's name to "Book Makers & Dreamers." Then she raised the question of content. What should the book be about? The kids thought a book about veggies and a talking refrigerator sounded like fun. Sawyer balked.

"A big book should make a big statement," I told them.

Nothing about their club was ever little again.

She had them talk about the things they thought most about. It wasn't long after 9/11; many students talked about fear, terrorism, and how could the world be made more safe and peaceful. This, the group decided, would be the book's subject. They each wrote their own thoughts, and then, at Sawyer's suggestion, decided to ask Nobel Peace Prize winners, as well as other leaders and children around the world, to share theirs.

"Remember, these are very, very busy people," Sawyer cautioned her students. "They may not get back to you."

But they did. From the Dalai Lama and Nelson Mandela, to Maya Angelou, Jimmy Carter, and Ted Kennedy, as well as from other school kids around the world, the letters began coming back. Then they began filling boxes. A T-shirt with the project's logo ("Big Book For Peace") traveled on a NASA shuttle to the International Space Station. (One of the astronauts had two nephews at the school.)

The group was invited to come to New York and speak at a special UN meeting. When we visited the school in 2009, there was no mistaking the mounting excitement of the students. But what was exciting and fun was also bumping up against more sobering realities: Making a one-ton book is not easy. Or cheap. And the odds are against it ever getting done at all. Plus, the project's original fifth-graders were now moving on to high school. (Although many remained involved in the project, coming after school to work alongside younger students.)

"God bless 'em, but it'll never get finished," I said to Carl, my photographer, driving home after one of our first visits to the school.

And but for Sawyer's unwavering optimism, it wouldn't have. "They know this book will get done, and they will see it done," she repeated like a mantra.

Luckily for the students, Sawyer's outsized optimism is matched by her dogged determination.

"Look, early on I don't think many people believed," says Sawyer matter-of-factly today.

So she made them believe. Tooling around town on her motorbike, she seemed to be everywhere, making sure parents and neighbors knew about the super-sized student project unfolding in their midst.

"I think they thought, 'There's that lady with the Big Book—we better find out what this is about and support her because she ain't going anywhere. . . .'"

Money was raised, a dollar or two at a time. A large, commercial printing company offered to print the pages on machines used normally for creating billboard-sized graphics. Another New England company that manufactured those huge printers donated hundreds of gallons of ink. The problem of what to actually print the pages themselves on (paper wasn't feasible) was solved when the DuPont Company donated what was discovered to be the perfect solution—rolls of its Tyvek material. The engineering department of a local college offered to design a huge, mechanized page-turner as part of its teaching curriculum. Friends came together to build a big, wooden book stand; others spent hours on their hands and knees punching hundreds of holes for the binding.

More than anything, Sawyer was determined that the project's original fifth-graders would see their after-school club dream fulfilled before they graduated and moved away. And on May 22, 2012, a school auditorium curtain parted, and however improbably, "The Big Book: Pages For Peace" was unveiled.

What had taken almost a decade and the combined efforts of teachers and nearly two hundred students, what had brought together the school, the town, and the business community in an effort that seemed at first like a grade school lark, was presented to a cheering gathering of all those same people, including the just-graduated seniors who had started it all. The Big Book stood on stage in a spotlight, surrounded by Sawyer and her cheering students. It towered over them, composed of one thousand pages drawn from three thousand letters and artwork from all over the world. It did indeed make a big statement. About sheer size, sure. But also about resolve, youthful idealism, and the extraordinary dedication of one remarkable teacher.

As it turns out, the students' Big Book was being completed at the exact same time I was completing this small book of my own. And in the same year that *Chronicle*—which aired the Big Book story originally—celebrated its thirtieth year

Turning a big page Photo Courtesy of *Chronicle*/WCVB-TV

of doing just such stories from around New England. I like all that symmetry. And symbolism. Because in its own way, the story behind the Big Book's unlikely creation captures much that is characteristic and true and timeless about New England itself. From something small and humble in stature, even as small as an idea, something grand and creative and inventive—even whimsical—is imagined. There are problems to solve, and obstacles to overcome—often with equal ingenuity. (Know where New England farmers got the stones to make the low walls that marked their land and kept their cows in pasture? From those same fields they had to get the stones *out of* to be able to farm in the first place.) And through a mix of sweat and guts and brains, hard work and determination, big things—and small—are achieved. Sometimes it's a big book made by young people. Sometimes it's a very, very small book made by an old man with only one good hand and one good eye. It's finding an ingenious way to memorialize an Old Man in the mountains who's loved but gone; and it's finding a way in the harbor to reclaim islands still there but long neglected. It's as simple as finding a way to do an everyday thing in an everyday place—an ice rink or a construction project—with pride and joy and dignity. It's finding the means to make other people laugh or watch in rapt attention. And sometimes, it's just enough to share the collection of stuff you've stayed true to since you were a kid, or the hot dogs you're passionate enough to put your name to.

Me? I get to tell and share these wonderful stories. And, even better—eat those hot dogs.

ACKNOWLEDGMENTS

There is a large and far-flung family of friends, colleagues, and other folks to thank for this book coming to completion. But the family I actually live with comes first. They encouraged me, supported my efforts, put up with my absences, and were patient and pulled for me throughout. Without that love and home field advantage from my wife, Anne Marie, and my daughters, Kyra and Daisy, I might still be struggling. (With the book, too.) My wife (herself a former journalist) was the first person to read a word I'd written. Her insightful feedback was invaluable; her belief to begin with even more so. Thank you. My daughters would often ask, "Are we in the book, dad?" You are now, girls.

I'm also very grateful for the support that *Chronicle*'s executive producer, Chris Stirling, and managing editor Susan Sloane extended to me from the beginning. While broadcast journalism in the field is increasingly a solo operation, *Chronicle* is still a blessedly collaborative effort. Which means that virtually none of the stories I've done would have been possible without working alongside some of the most talented professionals anywhere. Mine is, after all, a visual medium, so how fortunate for me that photographers like Carl Vieira, Bob Oliver, and Judi Guild made the pictures that told my stories. Skilled editors like Joe Mozdiez, Ellen Boyce, and Debbie Therrien took those pictures and my writing and crafted them into fully finished pieces. And without Art Donahue, a masterful photographer and editor both, well, I'd still be stumbling through some of the more technical aspects of putting those pictures all together here—thank you, Art.

Thanks as well at WCVB to general manager Bill Fine, Leona McCarthy, Russ Nelligan, Richard Feindel, and Bryan Kelleher. Thanks also to Liz Cheng at WGBH-TV, Boston.

Of course, before I could share these stories, first on *Chronicle* and then here, we needed the cooperation of those whose stories they are to begin with. Thank you to each of you who allowed us into your homes and into your lives for a brief time.

While many of this book's photographs originated on *Chronicle,* others are the work of truly talented professional photographers from around New England who were generous and kind in supporting my effort. Thanks in particular to Mark Kanegis, Jack Rowell, Meg Birnbaum, Jeb Wallace-Brodeur, and Vera Kaufman. Thanks, also, to the Norman Rockwell Family Agency.

I am very grateful as well to my former colleague Peter Mehegan. I could hardly have written about Maine without checking in with Pete.

Thank you to Globe Pequot Press, and to my wonderful editors, Erin Turner, Courtney Oppel, and Tracee Williams for their patience, professionalism, and prompt and helpful response to every question I raised, dumb, naïve, or otherwise.

Finally, it must be noted that while *Chronicle* is beloved by many and fiercely committed to by its staff, it is nonetheless something of a vanishing species—the opportunity to still do long-format feature stories on television has mostly disappeared. Yet New Englanders keep reminding us that they rather like this particular anachronism. It seems to be a faith that the show and the region it's devoted to have kept with each other for more than three decades.

So a fitting and final "Thank you" to our friends around New England. There is truly no place like home.

New Harbor Fog, New Harbor, Maine Photo by Vera Kaufman

ABOUT THE AUTHOR

Since 1997, Ted Reinstein has been a reporter for *Chronicle,* WCVB-TV/Boston's award-winning—and America's longest-running, locally produced—nightly news-magazine. In addition, he is a regular contributor for the station's political round-table show, writes a weekly online opinion column, and sits on WCVB's Editorial Board. In 2002, he was part of a team that won a national DuPont-Columbia Broadcast Journalism Award for *Chronicle*'s coverage of Boston's Big Dig project. Elsewhere on TV, he has hosted the *Popular Mechanics Show* for the Discovery Channel, and explored volcanoes in Hawaii and the islands of Tahiti for the Travel Channel's photo/adventure series *FreezeFrame.* He is coauthor of the play *Yom Kippur in Da Nang,* and has contributed several shorter plays for Boston's annual Theatre Marathon. A native New Englander, he's proud to know who makes the best clam chowder, as well as who's the only person ever to pinch-hit for Ted Williams. He lives just west of Boston with his wife and two daughters.

Photo Courtesy of *Chronicle*/WCVB-TV